Making Numbers Make Sense

A Sourcebook
for Developing Numeracy

Ron Ritchhart

Addison-Wesley Publishing Company

Menlo Park, California ∎ Reading, Massachusetts ∎ New York ∎ Don Mills, Ontario
Wokingham, England ∎ Amsterdam ∎ Bonn ∎ Sydney ∎ Singapore ∎ Tokyo ∎ Madrid ∎ San Juan
Paris ∎ Seoul ∎ Milan ∎ Mexico City ∎ Taipei

To my students, colleagues, mentors, and companions—your encouragement is such a special gift. Thank you.

This book is published by Innovative Learning™, an imprint of Addison Wesley's Alternative Publishing Group.
Managing Editor: Michael Kane
Project Editor: Katarina Stenstedt
Production: Karen Edmonds
Design Manager: Jeff Kelly
Text and Cover Design: Paula Shuhert
Cover Illustration: Stephanie Langley

ISBN 0-201-81749-7
2 3 4 5 6 7 8 9 10-ML-97 96 95 94 93

This Book Is Printed
On Recycled Paper

Contents

Introduction

Philosophy

Mathematics is not about numbers, but about making numbers make sense. The student who can work flexibly with numbers and reason with numerical information can appreciate mathematics as a tool for solving problems and interpreting events. Numeracy, or mathematical literacy, is this ability to make sense out of numerical information. Developing numeracy, encouraging positive attitudes toward math, and promoting a sense of efficacy in students through the use of active investigations that use numbers in context are what this book is all about.

Making Numbers Make Sense supports the goals outlined by the National Council of Teachers of Mathematics (NCTM) in the *Curriculum and Evaluation Standards* through its focus on the development of students' problem-solving and reasoning abilities. In addition, the promotion of investigative teaching and classroom discourse found throughout *Making Numbers Make Sense* supports the NCTM's vision of teaching outlined in *Professional Standards*.

Purpose

The goal of this book is to support teachers who are seeking to change the way they and their students approach mathematics. This book provides instructional guidance and a collection of lesson plans and blackline masters for the elementary and middle school classroom. Each lesson is designed to engage students in making sense out of numbers and foster their ability to reason mathematically. Taken as a whole, the lessons provide a foundation for the development of numeracy.

Connections. Knowing how mathematics connects to other disciplines and how the strands of mathematics connect to each other is crucial to the development of numeracy. Connections do not happen by chance, but are the result of a deliberate effort by the teacher. In this book, suggestions are provided for helping students to connect mathematical ideas and make links with other subject areas including science and reading. Many of the lessons in the book suggest literature as an extension or as part of the lesson. A bibliography of children's literature related to numeracy can be found in the References section.

Active Construction of Meaning. The lessons in this book place an emphasis on students' active construction of meaning. At times, this is accomplished through the use of hands-on materials, or manipulatives, that are used to promote the visualization, formation, and internalization of new concepts. However, many of the lessons are abstract and call on students to construct meaning not from manipulatives but through an examination of their own reasoning and the reasoning of others. The lessons require active participation and group cooperation.

How to Use This Book

The first two chapters, "Ideas" and "Methods," develop the concept of numeracy and outline specific teaching strategies. These chapters provide a strong background for the successful teaching of the lessons in the book and other lessons that you may devise or adapt.

The third chapter, "Lessons," contains thirty-five lessons that may be used in any order to

■ Introduce a topic

■ Spark a series of investigations

■ Reinforce concepts

■ Assess students' abilities to apply concepts

1

The lessons are organized according to their level of abstraction, beginning with numbers related directly to the individual, progressing to concrete models, and finally moving to abstract representations. These lessons cover a wide variety of topics and levels. The Strands and Grade-Level Chart on page 164 serves as a quick reference for the mathematical strands covered in each lesson and suggests appropriate grade levels.

Because of the investigative nature of these lessons, they can be applied to a wide variety of grade levels. Older students will explore the topic in greater depth than younger ones. While some students may have mastered the concepts involved in a lesson, applying and investigating these concepts may prove far more challenging. The real-world quality of many of the lessons makes them an excellent motivational tool for older students who do not enjoy math or are experiencing difficulty. Each teacher will be the best judge of the appropriateness of a lesson for his or her students. Adaptations and modifications of lessons to meet students' needs are encouraged.

The fourth chapter, "Assessing Learning," provides a variety of alternative assessment ideas including classroom-ready observational checklists, interview questions, sample test items, and portfolios. The topic of what needs to be assessed as students develop numeracy is carefully addressed and forms the backdrop for the assessment strategies presented. Reporting students' progress to parents is also included along with a sample report form.

The fifth chapter, "Projects: Highlighting Numeracy," gives ideas for making the concept of numeracy a whole-school emphasis. These include ways to construct models of large numbers or engage in data analysis through a schoolwide census project.

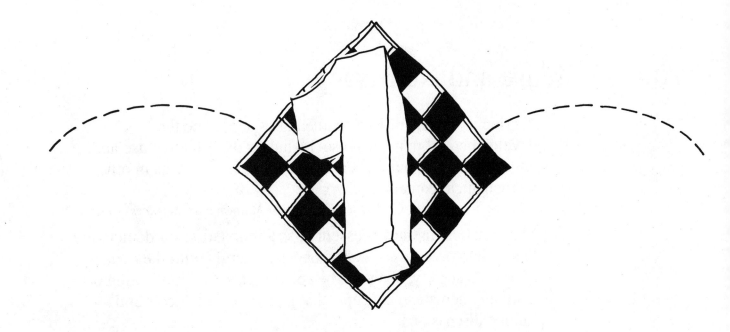

Ideas

Defining Terms

Number Sense and Numeracy

A principal theme of K–8 mathematics should be the development of number sense, including the effective use and understanding of numbers and applications as well as in other mathematical contexts.

Conference Board of the Mathematical Sciences (1982, p. 2)

Mathematical literacy is essential as a foundation for democracy in a technological age . . . To cope confidently with the demands of today's society, one must be able to grasp the implication of many mathematical concepts that permeate daily news and routine discussions.

National Research Council, Everybody Counts *(1989, pp. 7–8)*

Number sense first takes form as a rich collection of mental images of numbers built on concrete personal experiences. As adults, we have images of certain numbers. We can look at five objects and recognize that they have a quantity of five, but young children may have to count and even re-count the objects before they know the quantity. When someone talks about buying a dozen eggs, walking three miles, or attending an event with thousands of people, these numbers have meaning for us because we are able to reconstruct mental images of these quantities based on our experiences. For children who do not yet have a wealth of quantitative experiences to draw upon, these numbers lack meaning or sense. For adults, numbers like 250 million (the approximate population of the United States) or 1 billion (the approximate population of China) may have no meaning, as most adults only have limited experience with numbers of this magnitude. Building an understanding of such large numbers moves beyond number sense to the concept of numeracy or mathematical literacy.

Number sense involves the formation of relationships between numbers and an understanding of their relative magnitudes, for example, recognizing that six is simultaneously half a dozen, four less than ten, a nickel and a penny, and twice as much as three. The richer these relationships between numbers, the greater the comfort level and facility with which the individual can work. Building these kinds of relationships should be an ongoing goal of a curriculum designed to foster numeracy.

Children with good number sense feel comfortable with numbers and recognize the ways in which they can be used: to quantify (determining how many), to identify location (as with room numbers, addresses, and ZIP codes), to order objects (as in labeling first, second, third . . .), and to measure (as when determining height, length, weight, or age).

These components of number sense are reiterated in the NCTM's *Curriculum and Evaluation Standards for School Mathematics* (1989, p. 38), which outlines five components of number sense: "Children with good number sense (1) have well-understood number meanings, (2) have developed multiple relationships among numbers, (3) recognize the relative magnitudes of numbers, (4) know the relative effect of operating on numbers, and (5) develop referents for measures of common objects."

Numeracy expands the concept of number sense to include mathematical concepts such as chance, logic, and statistics. Like literacy, numeracy involves the ability to read and interpret information: quantitative information.

Numeracy encompasses the idea of number sense. It is, however, a more far-reaching term. Unfortunately, the idea of number sense is too often confined to the prearithmetic work done by students in kindergarten and first grade. The concept of numeracy has the advantage of being relatively new and thus more easily applied to all levels of mathematical learning from kindergarten to adult. Due to its broader scope, the term numeracy is used here to denote both number sense and general mathematical literacy.

Innumeracy

Innumeracy, an inability to deal comfortably with the fundamental notions of number and chance, plagues far too many otherwise knowledgeable citizens.

John Allen Paulos, Innumeracy *(1988, p. 3)*

The evidence of innumeracy abounds. In his book *Innumeracy* (1988), John Allen Paulos points to the popularity of lotteries, the proliferation of pseudoscience, and the misuse and misinterpretation of statistics. As teachers, we each have our own anecdotal evidence of innumeracy. An analysis of the National Assessment of Educational Progress (NAEP) produces many examples. Students apply rote procedures without regard for the context of the problem. An example of this is the bus problem: if a bus holds 30 children, how many buses are needed to take 375 children on a field trip? A common answer is $12\frac{1}{2}$. While the computation is correct, an answer of $12\frac{1}{2}$ buses clearly doesn't work. Solving problems involves not only applying arithmetic skills but also considering the context in which the numbers are being used. Examples such as these indicate that "once students learn to rely on procedures, they tend to give up on common sense . . . . They no longer have any idea whether their answers are reasonable" (Dossey et al. 1988, p. 67).

We know a lot about how children develop the basic concept of number, largely from Piaget's landmark work some fifty years ago; yet many children and adults still lack basic numeracy. Why? "One contributing factor is that we teach as though symbols have obvious and inherent meaning" (California Department of Education 1987, p. 10). In many classrooms, students are not given the opportunity to construct their own meaning based on personal experiences. Much of students' early work in mathematics concentrates on developing computational skills rather than on rich activities that teach them "to deal flexibly with numbers and move from one operation to another with equal skill" (Baratta-Lorton 1976, p. 66). For many students, this overemphasis on computation results in the meaningless manipulation of symbols, without understanding. If students lack understanding of a concept, no amount of practice or mastery of a skill will produce it.

Attention to developing number relationships is often brief and may occur only in the primary grades. Driven by the phantom of standardized tests, teachers and principals often make the conscious or unconscious decision to stress skills above understanding. However, this need not be an either-or situation.

Throughout their school careers students need the opportunity to work with and interpret numerical information. Graphing, estimating, and measurement should permeate the curriculum in order to give students the opportunity to work with real and meaningful numbers. This provides the context in which students can engage in natural computational activities to develop their skills. Concrete models of numbers must not stop with hundreds and thousands but need to be extended to millions and beyond in order to provide students with a sense of what these numbers mean.

Some Facts

We live in a country of approximately 250 million people with a $3 trillion debt and annual deficits exceeding $200 billion. Large numbers have become a part of our daily existence. Incomes in the tens of millions of dollars are not uncommon for CEOs, movie stars, and sports celebrities. Gross national products, movie grosses, and populations often reach hundreds of millions or even billions. Large numbers have become commonplace in our society, especially in dealing with monetary figures.

In the history of mathematics, the need for very large numbers has occurred only recently. In the thirteenth century the word *million,* meaning "great thousand," was first recorded. However, it was not until the seventeenth century that the word *million* began to take precedence over the more common *thousand thousand.* Only in the twentieth century have the words *million, billion,* and *trillion* entered into common usage.

In the American numeration system each denomination above a thousand is one thousand times the preceding denomination. A million is a thousand thousand, a billion is a thousand million, a trillion is a thousand billion, and so on. Each comma in a written number corresponds to a new denomination name. It is necessary for an informed citizenry to have a good understanding of the relative magnitudes of such large numbers as they become more commonplace.

The American numeration system is the same as the French. However, the British and German systems differ from ours in that they use the term *milliard* to represent one thousand million (our billion, or ten to the ninth power), *billion* to represent one million million (our trillion, or ten to the twelfth power), and each subsequent denomination is one million times the last.

The following chart provides the American names for denominations of one million and above.

AMERICAN DENOMINATIONS

Name	Value in Powers of 10	Number of Zeros	Number of Commas
Million	10^6	6	2
Billion	10^9	9	3
Trillion	10^{12}	12	4
Quadrillion	10^{15}	15	5
Quintillion	10^{18}	18	6
Sextillion	10^{21}	21	7
Septillion	10^{24}	24	8
Octillion	10^{27}	27	9
Nonillion	10^{30}	30	10
Decillion	10^{33}	33	11
Undecillion	10^{36}	36	12
Duodecillion	10^{39}	39	13
Tredecillion	10^{42}	42	14
Quattuordecillion	10^{45}	45	15
Quindecillion	10^{48}	48	16
Sexdecillion	10^{51}	51	17
Septendecillion	10^{54}	54	18
Octodecillion	10^{57}	57	19
Novemdecillion	10^{60}	60	20
Vigintillion	10^{63}	63	21

The largest named numbers in mathematics are a *googol*, which is represented by a 1 with 100 zeroes after it, or 10^{100}, and a *googolplex*, which is represented by a 1 with a googol of zeros after it, or 10^{googol}. These figures are so large that nothing exists (not even atoms) that they can be used to quantify.

While the terms for big numbers are often fun for students to learn and can spark much interesting discussion, simply knowing a number name or even writing a symbol does not make numbers meaningful, no more than a four-year-old's rote counting indicates an understanding of what those numbers mean. Just as the four-year-old must attach meaning to the words through concrete experiences, models, and applications, so too must older children engage in meaningful activities, construct models, and engage in applications to develop their numeracy as it relates to large numbers.

Numbers quickly grow too large to actually construct models, however. A model of one million one-centimeter cubes would be a cubic meter. Constructing such a model is a practical and useful task for children. However, constructing a model of a billion one-centimeter cubes would be roughly equivalent to constructing a 2-story building as wide and deep as it is tall. Furthermore, a model of a trillion cubes would consist of a 25-story building with a base of 350 square feet. Comparisons such as these, in the absence of actual models, can make large numbers meaningful.

Averaging also provides a means of reducing large numbers to a scale that can be more easily understood. National budgets, deficits, and other government expenditures frequently reach billions and even trillions of dollars. In the United States, a budget deficit of $250 billion would translate to a shortfall of approximately $1,000 per person. A $4 trillion national budget would equate to a cost of approximately $16,000 per person. Numerate citizens can use this information to help make informed decisions and place policy decisions in a meaningful context in which they can be better understood.

A Brief History of Place Value

A firm understanding of place value is a prerequisite for all work in arithmetic. Students who do not understand the concept of place value cannot progress through the four basic operations without difficulty . . . . It is essential that place value be given major emphasis in the primary grades and that students have frequent experiences with manipulative materials that demonstrate place value.

California Department of Education, Mathematics Framework *(1985, p. 23)*

Place value is the term that describes the mathematical organizational system we use for expressing numbers greater than nine. Each digit in a number symbol takes on a "value" due to its position or "place" in that symbol. For example, in the number 258, the 5 represents five groups of ten, whereas in the number 345, the 5 represents five ones. The Hindu-Arabic system of numeration we use allows us to express any number through the proper positioning of the ten basic digits 0, 1, 2, 3, 4, 5, 6, 7, 8, and 9.

Ancient Numbering Systems

Other systems of numeration, such as the ancient Chinese, Egyptian, or Roman systems, used a specific symbol for each denomination. The Roman system used the symbol I to represent one, X to represent ten, and C to represent one hundred. These symbols were repeated and combined in an appropriate way to indicate quantities. For example, twenty-three would be expressed as XXIII. Such a system is far more concrete (the two tens and three ones are clearly discernible), but far more cumbersome.

While these systems use the same base-ten groupings as the Hindu-Arabic system, the position of symbols does not affect the denomination. In the original Roman system, both IX and XI were used to represent eleven. The subtractive and additive aspect of the system in which IX came to mean 10 – 1 and XI to mean

10 + 1 came later. Even so, positioning does not affect the denomination ("I" always indicates one), only whether the number was to be added or subtracted.

The ancient abacus further facilitated movement toward a place-value system. On the abacus each successive column of beads represents the next power of ten. Numbers are represented by pushing the appropriate number of beads toward the center bar. The beads above the bar have a value five times that of the ones below the bar. The quantity 207 would be represented as follows:

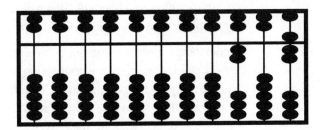

The abacus clearly uses placement to determine value, the far right column being the ones, followed by the tens, hundreds, thousands, and so on. However, the abacus is a computational tool and is not used for recording numbers. It made work with large numbers much easier, but the writing or recording of numbers was still difficult.

The most significant difference between these ancient systems and our current one is the absence of a place holder in the ancient systems. Whenever a specific symbol is used to represent denominations there is no need to show the absence of a particular denomination. For example, CCCI in the Roman system would denote 301. There is no need to indicate that there are no groups of ten; the absence of any X symbols is obvious. Similarly, on the abacus the absence of a denomination is apparent from the lack of beads pushed toward the center counting bar. In a place-value system the absence of any denomination must be made explicit. There is a clear difference between 47, 407, and 4007 in our current system.

Place Value

Without a place-value system it is extremely cumbersome to write or read large numbers. Our place-value system allows for the compact recording of large quantities using only ten digits. While the system is ingenious, and facilitated enormous discoveries in the field of mathematics, it presents unique difficulties for young children in their initial development of numeracy.

Our number system is more abstract than the ancient systems (in which specific symbols were used to represent denominations) making it more difficult for young children to read and write numerals greater than ten. Furthermore, in the English language the numbers zero through twelve each have their own unique names, having little relationship to one another. However, only the numbers zero through nine have their own unique symbols. Ten, eleven, and twelve are represented by combining digits using the place-value system.

The concept of zero as a place holder or indicator of an empty set is crucial in writing numbers correctly, and once again our language makes this difficult. We say "two hundred seven," leaving out any mention of the tens. Yet we must write the numeral as 207, clearly indicating that there are no tens. For young students this concept of an empty set is a giant step in mathematical understanding, and it is not made easier by our language.

In the ancient systems and on the abacus it was possible, though not necessary, to use more than nine of any denomination. Fourteen tens could be recorded by using fourteen Xs, and the quantity would still be readily understood since the Xs clearly stood for ten. In our place-value system, however, one may not have more than nine of any denomination. We cannot write eighty-five as seven tens and fifteen ones without the use of labels ("7 tens, 15 ones") for fear it would be confused with seven hundred fifteen. Thus, we must teach the process of regrouping in order to facilitate number understanding, writing, and operations.

Understanding place value is a difficult task for young students because their experience has emphasized connecting concrete objects with rote counting. Young students rely on the patterns in the counting sequence (twenty-one, twenty-two . . . thirty-one, thirty-two . . .) to help them figure out what comes next and which is larger. It is quite a leap for them to realize that digits change value depending upon their position. A student may be able to count to a hundred but might read the number 32 as "three two."

Developing a feel for place value requires concrete experiences in grouping objects. Working with groups other than ten is helpful in developing the concept of grouping and place value, but young students need numerous experiences grouping in sets of ten to realize the basis for our numeration system. Their work with grouping objects should move from concrete materials, to making a record of their concrete work, to abstract experiences with symbols. Often students are moved too rapidly to work with abstract symbols, creating confusion about numbers and operations with numbers. Questions like, Do we carry? Am I supposed to regroup? are indications that place-value concepts are not well-rooted. An understanding of place value is critical if students are to comprehend the relative magnitudes of large numbers when they are encountered in print.

Methods

Developing a Knowledge of Numbers

Investigations

> We learn mathematics particularly well when we are actively
> engaged in creating not only the solution strategies but the
> problems that demand them.
>
> *Moses et al. (1990, p. 90)*

> As students communicate their ideas, they learn to clarify, refine,
> and consolidate their thinking.
>
> *National Council of Teachers of Mathematics (1989, p. 6)*

Learning mathematics involves investigations. An investigative approach revolves
around the central question, "What can we find out about _____?" Investigations
move students beyond problem solving to problem posing when they are able to
build on their knowledge and explore questions that are important to them as
individuals. Students can construct meaning from such experiences.

When students are given the opportunity to pursue their unique problems and
solutions, your role and expectations as a teacher must shift. No longer a dispenser
of facts and the ultimate authority, you must model posing problems and asking
questions that engage students in thinking mathematically rather than recalling
answers. You must begin to pose problems that will engage not only your students,
but you as well. When the classroom becomes a community of learners, a climate of
trust and inquiry is formed. The use of open-ended questioning, the positive recog-
nition of efforts, and a focus on the thinking process rather than on final answers
help facilitate the creation of such a climate.

Many of the lessons in this book present students with the opportunity to investigate
problems in their own way and provide a context for further exploration and
problem posing. After teaching the lesson "Weighing Pennies," give the class the
opportunity to design new explorations. Some students might suggest repeating the
weighing activities with more pennies, others might suggest keeping the ten pennies
but using them to measure length, still others might want to figure out the total
number of pennies in the whole class. Allow students to explore their individual
problems, self-select groups to explore different problems, or have the class choose
a problem to explore. The original lesson provides the students with background
knowledge and serves as a springboard for continued discoveries.

Mathematics is a social activity. Students solidify their knowledge through actively
reflecting on their experiences, and independent investigation is not sufficient.
Question students in a way that requires them to analyze and synthesize
information. Prod students into posing new questions and designing investigations
of their own: How did you solve that? What do you think would happen if you did
_____? What does _____ have to do with this problem? Is this like any other
problem you've worked? What have you found so far?

Closure is an important component of any lesson. Students must be given the opportunity to share their discoveries and deal directly and honestly with challenges from others. By articulating what they have learned, students link their understanding to previous knowledge. Debriefing is an important aspect of all the lessons in this book; without it, the lessons are reduced to fun activities rather than being rich learning experiences.

Investigations should be a regular and integral part of a mathematics curriculum that seeks to develop numeracy. They provide firsthand experiences with numbers in a meaning-rich environment. Drill and practice have their place in solidifying procedures after concepts are understood, but they should not characterize students' mathematical experiences. When the practice of skills is needed, the practice itself should be of a problem-solving nature. In the lesson "The Rounding Game," students are given the opportunity to practice their rounding skills while employing strategy in playing the game. They can share their strategies and offer up their own modifications of the game during the class discussion.

Algorithms

Education is not merely the transmission of information. . . . We need instead to construct for ourselves (and for the children in our charge) patterns with which to make sense of the world. We must sell understanding, not information. We must be wise, not just smart.

Robert W. Cole, Jr. (1987)

The weakness of our schools as documented in the National Assessment of Educational Progress (NAEP) is not that our students cannot do arithmetic, it is that they cannot think mathematically. The cause of this phenomenon is not hard to uncover: curriculums are driven by standardized tests, which emphasize rote mechanical skills in arithmetic almost totally divorced from mathematical thinking and understanding. A mathematics curriculum based on teaching the algorithms for computation is really no curriculum at all. We must question seriously any elementary education focused exclusively on computational skills. Such an education produces individuals less efficient and reliable than a five-dollar calculator.

In traditional elementary schooling, computational skills are emphasized through the teaching of algorithms. An algorithm is any procedure that can be carried out as a means of achieving a desired result. We have algorithms for many of the routine tasks we perform daily such as starting the car, getting dressed in the morning, or cooking a meal. Algorithms exist in mathematics as well. The set of procedures that we apply in adding two-digit numbers is an algorithm. The way in which we perform long division is an algorithm.

For most of us, these algorithms were learned through repeated practice of the procedure until they became automatic. We do not need to understand how or why the algorithm works to apply it. We need know nothing about combustion or mechanics to start our car. We do not have to learn chemistry to bake chocolate chip cookies, nor do we need to grasp anything about numbers or mathematics to successfully apply computational algorithms, and therein lies the rub.

Unfortunately, many teachers, both elementary and secondary, believe that teaching mathematics consists only of demonstrating algorithms and providing ample opportunity for practice. Textbooks, tests, and our own experiences reinforce this type of teaching, and it is a difficult cycle to break. When the emphasis of the curriculum is mimicry, children's ability to develop numeracy is suppressed. In fact, numeracy can become totally subjugated to the repetition of meaningless procedures. "To learn a method by rote is of little value; only when it is given a full justification, and the reasons for the steps established, can anyone benefit" (Buxton 1984). In such instances, the lucky students will be those who are able to meaningfully connect and understand these procedures on their own or with a skilled teacher at some later date. The unlucky students, of whom there are many, will continue in their belief that math is a mystery.

"Good" teachers have traditionally been those who were able to demonstrate the algorithms effectively. They employed manipulatives and built an understanding of place value that students could use as a base for making sense of the algorithm. In such a setting, students' developing numeracy is not interrupted and may even be reinforced. However, we must question the wisdom of continuing to devote so much of our time and energy to explicitly teaching these computational algorithms at all. We must examine to what extent this type of teaching may actually inhibit children's ability to think mathematically.

While I would suggest that the current emphasis on computation be lessened, I am not advocating that computation no longer be taught in the elementary curriculum. Rather, it is the teaching of mathematical algorithms that must be addressed. It is naively assumed by most teachers and Americans in general that the algorithms we learned and now teach possess some special type of mathematical correctness, validity, and truth, and that the precise and uniform execution of these algorithms is necessary for future work in mathematics. It is this universally held and erroneous assumption that speaks to the inefficiency and uniformity of both past and current teaching. It may also account for the negative attitudes about math and the general innumeracy of our society.

Many of us assume that the way we were taught to perform addition, subtraction, multiplication, and division are the only ways in which these operations are to be executed. In reality, the algorithms that we use are but a few of many possible algorithms. Algorithms differ historically and by culture, and all are equally valid and reliably produce accurate results. Let's examine a few of these in subtraction:

Traditional

Our traditional algorithm for subtraction is often called decomposition, as we decompose the minuend to permit us to subtract in the ones column. This decomposition is often referred to as regrouping, trading, or borrowing.

$$\begin{array}{r} {\scriptstyle 12}\ \ {\scriptstyle 5} \\ \cancel{6}\ \cancel{2} \\ -4\ 7 \\ \hline 1\ 5 \end{array}$$

minuend

subtrahend

difference

Equal Additions of Ten	In the equal additions of tens algorithm, the ones in the minuend are increased by ten as the tens in the subtrahend are increased by ten. We can determine that this procedure is	$\begin{array}{r} 6\,\overset{12}{\cancel{2}} \\ -\,\overset{5}{\cancel{4}}\,7 \\ \hline 1\,5 \end{array}$

mathematically valid in that $62 - 47 = 72 - 57$. It is the placement of the added ten that makes the subtraction process more manageable.

Equal Additions

In the equal additions algorithm, both the minuend and subtrahend are increased by the same amount added to the ones in order to produce a subtraction problem in which decomposition is not necessary. The quantity to be added is determined by the difference of the subtrahend and the

$$\begin{array}{r} 6\,2_{\,+3} \\ -4\,7_{\,+3} \\ \hline 1\,5 \end{array} \longrightarrow \begin{array}{r} 6\,5 \\ -5\,0 \\ \hline 1\,5 \end{array}$$

next multiple of ten. In this instance, $50 - 47 = 3$. Thus, the quantity 3 is added to both the minuend and the subtrahend. Again, we can see that these are mathematically equivalent: $62 - 47 = 65 - 50$.

Complementary

In the complementary method, the subtraction is actually changed to an addition problem. This method was popular during the eighteenth and nineteenth centuries. In this method, the complement of the subtrahend is added to the minuend. The complement is the difference between a number and the next higher power of ten: 3 is the complement of 7, 62 is the complement of 38, and so on. In the resulting sum, the lead digit "1" is eliminated to produce the answer to the original subtraction exercise.

This method can be shown to work algebraically:

$$\begin{array}{r} 6\,2 \\ -4\,7 \\ \hline 1\,5 \end{array} \qquad \begin{array}{r} 6\,2 \\ +5\,3 \\ \hline 1\,1\,5 \end{array}$$

State the original exercise as $A - B = C$.

The complement of B is $100 - B$.

Add the complement of B to the minuend:

$A + (100 - B)$

Reorder using the associative property:

$(A - B) + 100$

Substitute C for $A - B$, as $A - B = C$:

$C + 100$

Remove the lead digit, in this case 100:

C

Since all these methods are equally valid, the decision of which one if any to teach is primarily a cultural and historical one. Surprisingly, considerable research indicates that it is not necessary to teach any algorithm at all for students to learn to compute quickly and efficiently. Students are able to create their own algorithms to solve addition and subtraction problems (Kamii 1989).

When students' work has focused on developing numeracy and they have a strong sense of number and place value, they possess the skills needed to create their own algorithms, which are often more efficient than traditional algorithms. In the lesson "Tiles in Our Shoes," students estimate and count the tiles needed to fill their shoes. In their counting, they are encouraged to group the tiles by tens. Finally, students form groups of three with other classmates and determine the total number of tiles used by all three. When I taught this lesson in several first grade classrooms, I watched closely to see how the students would solve this problem, or whether it would be beyond their grasp. The students in the different classrooms approached the problem with striking uniformity. Each student came to the group with the number of tiles he or she had used (a two-digit number) recorded. After their initial sharing and comparisons, students universally focused on the tens and counted the total number of tens used by all three individuals. Some experienced difficulty in moving from counting by tens to hundreds. Some groups reported 13 tens rather than 1 hundred and 3 tens, or 130. Next, students turned their attention to the ones, grouping them to make tens as needed. These were added, usually mentally, to their previous partial sum for the total.

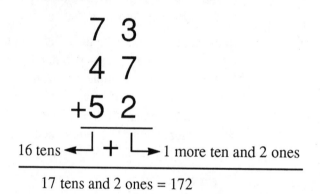

The lack of an algorithm didn't impede students at all. They were only hindered by their incomplete understanding of place value or basic addition facts. However, most possessed strategies for deriving the addition facts though they had not memorized "the facts."

The strategy that these first graders applied is fairly universal among young children given the opportunity to create their own algorithms (Kamii 1989). It even appears to be superior to the traditional algorithm in terms of mental computation.

In contrast to the first graders, I found that second graders had much more difficulty with the "Tiles in Our Shoes" lesson. Again, I presented the lesson in several second grade classrooms. When it came time to add the three groups of tiles, one student's comment typified many responses. He said, "We don't know how to do these kinds of problems yet." He knew from parents and siblings that there was a "correct" way to approach and solve double-digit addition. He was waiting to be told how to do it rather than using the knowledge he had already acquired about numbers and mathematics. This is the opposite of the response we should be seeking to elicit.

Building numeracy through meaningful experiences reduces, if not eliminates, the need to focus on computational algorithms. Rather than emphasizing "the" way of doing things, involve the class in explaining and discussing their original

Making Numbers Make Sense

approaches to computation. Give them opportunities to try out one another's algorithms. Finally, you can present the traditional algorithm as another alternative, not the correct and only way, and ask them to figure out why it works. Students do need to practice their computational skills to develop proficiency, but this practice should not be mindless mimicry. Have them practice a single algorithm that makes sense to them, is efficient, and is reliable within the context of authentic mathematical tasks and engaging games.

The most frequently asked questions at this point are: But what about next year's teacher? Won't the children be confused if next year they are told to do it the traditional way? The answer is no. Allowing students to invent their own algorithms and learn from one another builds their numeracy and gives them confidence in their ability to think mathematically. If your students have seen the traditional algorithm and analyzed it to see why it works, they will enter the next grade realizing that math is something they can reinvent and understand. They will not accept simply following the rules and will ask the teacher, Why do we do it this way?

We must also address the question of "next year's teacher" on a broader scale. Educators must address students' needs in the here and now, making all learning as meaningful and intrinsically motivating as possible. Curriculum cannot be based on the assumptions and beliefs of individuals who are themselves innumerate. We must make it our responsibility to educate these individuals, whether they be teachers or parents, about how children learn and about our own teaching practices. By de-emphasizing the teaching of algorithms, we will not decrease students' proficiency in computation. With meaningful practice of any algorithm, students will do well on standardized tests and should score even higher on their understanding of mathematical concepts when given the opportunity to think for themselves.

Numeracy involves having a feel for numbers and possessing an understanding of numbers and the meaningful relationships between them. With this as our goal, we must teach in a way that consistently allows and asks students to construct, develop, and build on their own understanding.

Connections

It is important that children connect ideas both among and within areas of mathematics. Without such connections, children must learn and remember too many isolated concepts and skills rather than recognizing general principles relevant to several areas. When mathematical ideas are also connected to everyday experiences, both in and out of school, children become aware of the usefulness of mathematics.

National Council of Teachers of Mathematics (1989, p. 32)

Connections do not happen by chance but are the result of a concerted effort on your part. Many types of connections need to take place during math instruction. Manipulatives must be related to the symbols and concepts they represent. Connections need to be made among the various content strands of mathematics. And connections need to be made between mathematics and other disciplines, such as science, social studies, and English.

Manipulatives are useful in mathematical learning in that they provide concrete models of abstract concepts and symbols. Work with manipulative materials alone does not provide students with an understanding of those concepts and symbols, however. You must select manipulatives that are a good model of the concept and appropriate for students' conceptual level.

For example, in developing an understanding of numbers, it is necessary for children to first develop one-to-one correspondence and the idea of conservation or invariance of number. One-to-one correspondence is the ability to match the rote number sequence (that is, 1, 2, 3, 4, 5 . . .), which most children memorize and can recite before entering school, to the counting of actual objects. Young children demonstrate one-to-one correspondence when they point to objects saying the next number in the counting sequence. Prior to this understanding, they may say the number sequence when pointing randomly at the objects being counted, demonstrating that the number names are not yet linked to the objects being quantified or counted. At this stage, it is important to give young students concrete objects to count. Once one-to-one correspondence is achieved, counting becomes a meaningful and useful activity. Until this point, number names, although known by the student, have no true meaning. The use of actual physical materials is crucial in developing this understanding prior to symbolic work with numbers.

Through continued counting experiences with concrete materials, students come to develop a concept of the invariance or conservation of number. This means they understand that no matter how a group of objects is arranged, the number of objects in the group never varies. Working with concrete materials allows students to make connections between the number words and their meanings.

When young students begin to explore place-value concepts, it is crucial that you select appropriate materials. Students must begin their understanding of place value by grouping objects together. At this stage they need to work with objects possessing a one-to-one correspondence (meaning that each object possesses a value of one), such as links, Unifix® Cubes, and beans. Students use these materials to form groups by making their own Unifix® trains, link chains, or bean sticks. Such experiences help them understand the process of grouping that underlies our place-value system.

Drawing on this understanding, students move on to materials possessing a predetermined structure and form, such as Cuisenaire® rods, Base Ten Blocks, and premade bean sticks. Earlier experiences with making their own groups enable students to understand and accept the structure imposed on these materials. Finally, they can work with abstract manipulatives, such as the chips in chip trading. In chip trading the materials are no longer grouped into sets of increasing value, and the value is not determined by the number of objects in the group but by the color of the chip. The connection between the chips, where the value is determined by color, and numerals, where the value is determined by the placement of the digits, needs to be made explicit. Do not assume that simply by working with the manipulatives students will make this connection on their own.

You must also help students to make a connection between these materials and the concepts they represent through work that involves recording symbolically on paper what was done with the manipulatives and discussing relationships that may be obvious to you but must be brought out for the students. You must clearly identify the purpose of the work with manipulatives and consciously move students forward toward the understanding of concepts, or else they may learn only to mimic procedures.

Geometry, measurement, numeration, number operations, statistics, probability, and logic are all related aspects of mathematics. Too often they are taught in a discrete and separate way when teachers attempt to cover the curriculum rather than uncover it. These strands need to be connected through the regular integration of topics rather than presented as separate units of study. The lessons in this book provide such connections. For example, the lesson "Handfuls" links measurement with graphing, numeration, and number operations. The lesson "Place-Value Graphing" combines logic, graphing, estimating, and place value. Such links allow students to view mathematics as a unified discipline rather than as isolated topics.

Connecting mathematics to other disciplines highlights its application and usefulness. Most students will not become true mathematicians, but all will use mathematics as a tool in their lives and careers. Yet often it is taught and learned apart from its usefulness and function. In the lesson "Richter Scale," students learn about logarithmic functions and exponential growth as they relate to measuring earthquakes. This makes a connection between mathematics and science as well as mathematics and our lives. Many of the lessons in this book include literature connections as extensions of the lessons. In addition, a bibliography of children's literature related to numeration can be found in the References section.

Estimation

Estimation interacts with number sense and spatial sense to help children develop insights into concepts and procedures, flexibility in working with numbers and measurements, and an awareness of reasonable results.

National Council of Teachers of Mathematics (1989, p. 36)

Estimation activities are valuable in developing and assessing students' grasps of both large and small numbers. Estimation is often taught as a discrete skill and not as a useful tool, however. Estimating the number of beans in a jar may be fun but is hardly a realistic situation. Furthermore, when you reward a student for getting the correct or closest answer, guessing rather than estimating is being reinforced. Such activities give the message that the point of estimating is to "hit" the actual amount. Instead of building numeracy, this undermines it. Later on, when asked to estimate the products before performing a multiplication problem, these students hesitate or change their estimate after doing the problem to avoid being "wrong." Try to refrain from rewarding actual guesses in estimating activities and refer to such guesses as lucky, but not any better than those within the reasonable range.

You need to make students aware of the purpose of estimation, when estimation is used, how to estimate, and how to judge the appropriateness of an estimate. Estimating provides a framework for judging the reasonableness of answers, whether done with pencil and paper or on a calculator. Emphasize this "range of reasonableness" whenever you ask students to estimate. The range of reasonableness depends on the situation. When estimating the number of people expected at a party, the host's estimate should be within a very small range. When estimating the voter turnout for an election, the range is much larger.

The amount of information one has is the major contributing factor in producing accurate estimates. The information can be on the most basic level; for example, knowledge of and previous experience with beans are helpful in estimating the number of beans in a jar. Information can be obtained from taking a sample, a procedure you should model and teach to students. When estimating the number of fish in a lake, scientists often take samples. Students should be given similar opportunities. In the lesson "Grains of Rice," students count the grains of rice in a small sample to help them arrive at an appropriate estimate. Taking samples allows students to work with and develop an understanding of proportionality and the magnitude of numbers.

Students are asked to estimate in many of the lessons in this book. This helps them to begin thinking numerically early in the lesson, practice their estimation skills, and devise a range of reasonableness to evaluate their work.

Measurement

Measurement provides a meaningful context in which to develop numeracy. Students need to see that measurement is done for a purpose, often to collect data or interpret situations quantitatively. Through measurement, they connect rote counting to concrete experiences and are exposed to fractions in a natural context. Measurement provides the opportunity to use numbers to quantify. Making comparisons between measurements provides a vehicle for connecting number order with number magnitude in a concrete manner. The language of comparison should be used: *more than/less than, taller/shorter, heavier/lighter, bigger/smaller.*

Have students measure weight, length, area, and volume in order to learn to recognize the contexts of measurement and to learn which units are appropriate for various tasks. Students' first experiences should be with nonstandard units of measure, such as paper clips, links, and beans. This develops measurement techniques and skills. In addition, through work with nonstandard units of measure, the need for a standard unit of measure emerges.

Graphing

Graphing and statistics are problem-solving tools that permeate our lives. Collecting, organizing, and analyzing data is a part of scientific research, industry, medicine, commerce, education, and government. Policy decisions affecting our lives are more and more frequently being based on the analysis of statistical information. Numerate individuals must be able to read and make sense of statistical information. They must be able to compose and decompose graphic information and have a clear grasp of the numbers being represented. Numerate individuals must understand what is meant by the terms *average, mean, median,* and *mode.*

Identifying what data to collect and how to gather and record it is the first step in this problem-solving process. Collecting data gives students firsthand experience with numbers. While gathering data, they are using their counting skills and establishing one-to-one correspondence.

The manner in which data is organized will subsequently determine what is "seen" and the conclusions that are drawn when analyzing the data. While organizing data, primary students are developing their classification skills as they determine which category to place information in. They are making a record of their findings. Upper elementary and middle school students use ratios, percentages, and the concept of scale to represent data more efficiently.

Analyzing data requires students to work with part-whole relationships, realizing that the sum of the parts must equal the whole. When analyzing data, students are making comparisons, drawing conclusions, and forming hypotheses. Through the process of analyzing data, they often devise new investigations they would like to carry out and explore.

The analysis of data is the most neglected component of graphing. Students are frequently asked to create graphs from data that has no relevance to them, or to "read" prepared graphs. Too often only the most perfunctory questions are asked: Which group has more? How many fewer does this group have than that? How many people were surveyed? True analysis means looking beyond the surface and asking questions that are inspired by the graph but not necessarily answered: If we did it again would we get the same result? If we surveyed a different grade level, would the graph change? Why do you think there are more of these than those? Would the graph be the same if we increased the sample? Questions such as these invite further investigations.

Primary students should have lots of practice with graphs, beginning with concrete experiences and leading to the abstract. Initially, have your students make real graphs using the actual objects they are sampling, move them on to pictorial graphs where pictures are used to represent the actual, and later have them make symbolic graphs in which symbols, such as check marks, replace both the pictures and the actual objects.

During their early experiences with graphing in kindergarten and first grade, students need to be exposed to the vocabulary of statistics. They should have no difficulty relating to the idea of the *mode,* the score or category that occurs most often in the graph. Figuring out which has the most is often a student's first observation when looking at a graph. While the term *mode* is more commonly used with numerical information, it can be used with nonnumerical information as well.

First and second graders can also understand that the word *range* is used to represent the difference between the lowest and highest measurements collected. For example, if the low temperature for the day was 65°F and the high was 84°F, then there was a range of 19°F.

In grades three and up, *median* and *mean* are useful terms to use in summarizing data. Both the median and the mean are measures of location. The median is the middle score in a distribution when the information is organized in numerical order. For example, when the number of school days missed during the year for each of twenty-five students in a class is graphed, it yields the following data:

0, 0, 0, 0, 0, 0, 0, 0, 1, 1, 2, 2, 3, 3, 3, 3, 3, 4, 4, 5, 5, 7, 9, 9, 15.

The median in this example is 3, since 3 represents the middle (or in this case the thirteenth) score in the distribution.

The mean, or average, is obtained by adding all the items in the distribution and dividing by the number of items. In the above example the average number of days absent would be 79 divided by 25, or 3.16 days. In this example, the mean and the median are very close. However, the mode in this example is further away, it is 0. The lesson "Average Height" provides a way of teaching about the terms *range, mode, median,* and *average (mean)* in a concrete manner before the formal algorithm is introduced.

Lessons

Teaching for Numeracy

Lessons

The lessons in this book are grouped into three categories: Numbers on a Human Scale, Working with Physical Models, and Abstracting and Extending. These categories represent the stages students pass through in developing numeracy. First, students need concrete experiences relating numbers to themselves and their world. Next, they need experience constructing and working with concrete models of numbers that can be internalized and used as points of reference when numbers are encountered in more abstract settings. Finally, students build on these understandings to engage in meaningful abstract work with numbers.

These groupings do not necessarily correspond to grade levels. While the lessons in Numbers on a Human Scale and Working with Physical Models are more suited to kindergartners through second graders, many are appropriate for third through eighth graders. The discerning characteristic is usually the magnitude of the numbers involved and the complexity of the concepts. Many activities designed for younger students can be used with older ones who lack numeracy at this level, or as initial investigations that can be extended.

Each lesson has three main components: the curricular component, the instructional component, and extensions.

The curricular component gives the topic, the mathematical strands that are incorporated in the lesson, and the materials that will be used. The strands used are a compilation taken from the NCTM's *Curriculum and Evaluation Standards* and the 1985 *Mathematics Framework for California Public Schools*. They are numeration, estimation, number operations, measurement, graphing, statistics, logic, algebra, and patterns. The strands provide a convenient way for you to link these lessons to your curriculum and explain to parents and administrators the purposes of the lesson. The materials used include Pattern Blocks, Color Tiles, links, equal-arm balances, rice, Cuisenaire® rods, pennies, dice, and calculators. In some cases, substitution of materials is possible. Recording sheets, overhead transparencies, and other printed materials are also listed. Many of the lessons in this book suggest the use of an overhead projector. While a chalkboard can often be substituted, the overhead projector has the advantage of keeping your focus toward the students and allows you to prepare materials in advance.

The instructional component of the lesson gives the conceptual level, the instructional level, and provides the actual description of the lesson in a step-by-step fashion, often suggesting appropriate questions for you to ask. The conceptual level for each lesson is either concrete, connecting, or abstract. Lessons at a concrete level indicate that students will be working strictly with manipulative materials, and no writing will be involved. Lessons at a connecting level provide a bridge from the concrete to the abstract. These lessons make use of concrete materials but also involve some written recording of students' work with the manipulatives. The connecting level helps students to make connections between the concepts represented by the materials and the abstract symbols. Lessons at the abstract level require students to work primarily with written symbols and may make some use of abstract manipulatives such as dice and calculators.

The instructional level is either exposure, practice, or mastery. The instructional level takes into account that learning occurs over time through the constructing of ideas on a personal level. Students should not be expected to master new concepts upon their introduction. Consequently, the majority of lessons that you teach should not be mastery lessons. Mastery is more often an ongoing process that students continue to move toward rather than a hurdle to pass.

Lessons at the exposure level provide students' first experiences with those concepts. The purpose is to expose students; mastery or even competency are not expected outcomes for these lessons. With further investigation of these ideas, students can begin to move toward mastery. Lessons at the practice level assume that students have had some experiences with these concepts and will therefore be practicing and reinforcing their skills during these lessons. Lessons at a mastery level assume students have had considerable practice and will move toward mastery during these lessons.

The instructional levels listed for these lessons are generalities. Any given lesson taught in a typical classroom may be at an exposure level for some of the students and at a practice level for others. Lessons initially taught at a practice level may subsequently be retaught for mastery. A lesson can be taught at an exposure level at one grade level and at a practice level at another grade level. Use your knowledge of your students to decide what levels the lesson will reach.

The description of each lesson begins with the purpose of the lesson. While every lesson in this book is designed to increase students' understanding and facility with numbers, each lesson does this in a unique way, which is explained. The majority of lessons in this book, and effective lessons in general, consist of three basic parts: modeling, action, and discussion. These three components may occur in any order. In lessons that stress new concepts, the usual sequence is modeling, action, and discussion. You model the concept or what is to be done. The students then perform the action that was modeled. Finally you help students reinforce their learning through discussion or writing. Lessons that stress problem-solving and application may begin with an activity where students seek solutions to the problem and end with a discussion and modeling of those solutions.

The extensions component of each lesson gives suggestions for further investigations and related activities. In some extensions, children's literature not mentioned in the lesson itself is listed to provide an opportunity to follow up and extend ideas encountered in the lesson. Having these books available in the room following a lesson provides an opportunity for interested students to explore their own ideas. Connections to other content areas are provided to assist you in planning integrated units.

Numbers
on a Human Scale

Handfuls

Strands

- Estimation
- Number Operations
- Graphing/Statistics

Materials

- Play money (quarters, dimes, nickels, pennies)
- One sock per child
- "Handfuls of Coins" recording sheet
- Coin graphing mat

Description of Lesson

Overhead projector   yes ☑   no ☐

Conceptual Level	Concrete ☐	Connecting ☑	Abstract ☐
Instructional Level	Exposure ☑	Practice ☐	Mastery ☐

Purpose

To practice estimating skills, generate data for informal addition and subtraction exercises, expose students to the difference model of subtraction, and use a counting on strategy in subtracting.

Students frequently receive much exposure to the take-away model of subtraction, which can limit their ability to use subtraction flexibly. The difference model, which receives less attention, involves comparing two quantities to determine the difference between the two. Counting the physical difference between these quantities is an effective strategy referred to as counting on. In this lesson, students employ the strategy naturally with physical objects, and later it can be translated to be used with a number line or mentally. To mentally determine the difference between 9 and 6 (9 – 6) using the counting on strategy, you would "count on" 7, 8, and 9, and keep track of the number of forward "steps" needed to reach 9.

Modeling

You may introduce this lesson by reading the book *My Hands* (Aliki 1990) to focus students' attention on their hands. Model steps 1, 2, and 3 for the class on the overhead projector or on the floor with students seated in a half circle around you. Discuss each action and ask the class to participate in the estimating, counting, and comparing.

Action

Step 1: Have students close their eyes, grab one handful of mixed play money, and place it in their sock without looking (they can work with partners to facilitate this). Even a first grader's hands can hold quite a few coins. You may want to have students use one-ounce scoops rather than their hands to make sure they get a smaller quantity. On their "Handfuls of Coins" recording sheets, students estimate the total number of coins they had in their handful as well as the number of each type of coin. Younger students should be allowed to feel their sock to facilitate their estimation.

Students' estimates provide a good assessment of who understands that the parts (the number estimated for each coin) must equal the whole (the total number of coins). This is an important prerequisite for the understanding of addition and subtraction. However, remember that students develop this understanding through experiences such as this rather than through being "told" or "corrected" by you.

Step 2: Have students dump their coins out of the socks and place them on their "Coin Graphing Mat" accordingly. The graphing mat provides a visual display so quantities may be compared easily. It facilitates counting and aids the development of the counting on strategy for subtraction.

Step 3: Have students record the actual amount of coins they have on their "Handfuls of Coins" recording sheets. Students use a number line to help figure the difference between their estimates and their actual number of coins. Some students will find this difficult as the numbers may not be presented in a consistent order on the graphing mat; the larger number may come first or second. It is therefore helpful to have a number line on which both numbers can be located and the difference between them counted. This exposes students to the difference model of subtraction and the counting on strategy.

Discussion

Each student's graph will be unique and will look different. Engage students in a variety of questions about their graphs:

Teacher: "Raise your hand if you have more than ten coins on your mat. Tell me how many more than ten you have" (call on individuals).

Student: "I have three."

Teacher: "If Mary has three more than ten, how many does she have?"

Student: "She has thirteen."

Teacher: "Raise your hand if you have less than ten coins. Tell me how many more you would need to make ten."

Student: "Two."

Teacher: "If John has two less than ten, how many does he have?"

Student: "Eight."

Teacher: "Raise your hand if you have more blues than greens. How many more blues do you have?"

Call on students to ask their own questions of the class.

▼ Extensions

- Repeat the lesson using a variety of materials: Color Tiles, Pattern Blocks, Cuisenaire® rods, and beans. A "Handfuls of Color Tiles" recording sheet and a graphing mat for Color Tiles are provided. The format of the lesson remains the same.

- Have students make symbolic representations of their graphs using check marks on separate graphing mats.

- Read the book *My Hands* (Aliki 1990) to students and encourage them to think of other ways to use their hands as measuring tools. The book also provides a way to integrate primary science skills into learning about the body.

Name _____

Handfuls of Coins

	Estimate	Actual	Difference
Quarters			
Dimes			
Nickels			
Pennies			
Total			

0   1   2   3   4   5   6   7   8   9   10   11   12   13

Coin Graphing Mat

8				
7				
6				
5				
4				
3				
2				
1				
	Quarters	Dimes	Nickels	Pennies

© Addison-Wesley Publishing Company, Inc.

Handfuls of Color Tiles

	Estimate	Actual	Difference
Red			
Green			
Yellow			
Blue			
Total			

0 1 2 3 4 5 6 7 8 9 10 11 12 13

Color Tile Graphing Mat

8				
7				
6				
5				
4				
3				
2				
1				
	Red	Yellow	Blue	Green

Paces

Strands

- Numeration
- Measurement

Materials

- Color Tiles
- Socks
- Construction paper

Description of Lesson

Overhead projector   yes ☐   no ☑

Conceptual Level	Concrete ☑	Connecting ☐	Abstract ☐
Instructional Level	Exposure ☑	Practice ☐	Mastery ☐

Purpose

To reinforce counting skills and grouping by ten while exposing students to the concept of perimeter and nonstandard units of measure.

Discussion

You may introduce this lesson by reading *My Feet* (Aliki 1990) to focus students' attention on the things their feet can do. Tell students that in this lesson, they will be using their feet to help them measure.

Action

Step 1: Have students take a walk around the school or a playing field dropping a Color Tile into their sock every time they count ten paces. Paces can be normal walking steps or toe-to-heel steps.

Step 2: Back in the room, students count their Color Tiles, saying 10, 20, 30, and so on. Have students trace their right feet on sheets of construction paper and cut them out. Then have them record their total number of steps on their construction-paper feet.

Discussion

Introduce the word *perimeter:* "When you walk or measure around the outside of something, we call the distance around the outside the perimeter. The perimeter is similar to a fence around the outer edge."

Collect data from the students: "When I call on you, would you please tell me how many paces it took for you to walk around the perimeter of the playground?"

Record each name and the number of paces on the chalkboard or overhead projector. Then ask, "Why did it take John more steps than Lisa to walk around the perimeter of the playground?"

The discussion should bring out the idea that the units of measurement (the paces) were not uniform. The lesson "The King's Foot" is a good follow-up to this lesson because it pursues the idea of a uniform system of measurement.

▼ Extensions

- Instead of tiles, students can use hundreds charts when counting and color them in row-by-row as they say the numbers.

- Students can select other distances to pace off, and record whether they are longer, shorter, or the same as their previous measurements.

- The construction-paper feet may be used as a bulletin-board display.

The King's Foot

Strands

- Numeration
- Estimation
- Measurement

Materials

- *How Big Is a Foot?* by Rolf Myller
- 12-inch rulers
- 1 × 9-inch strips of construction paper (one for each student)

Description of Lesson

Overhead projector   yes ☐   no ☑

Conceptual Level	Concrete ☑	Connecting ☐	Abstract ☐
Instructional Level	Exposure ☑	Practice ☐	Mastery ☐

Purpose

To expose students to the foot as a standard measure, develop measurement skill, provide an opportunity to make quantitative comparisons, and develop estimation skills using proportions.

Discussion

Read *How Big Is a Foot?* In this story problems arise when the king orders a bed to be built and gives the unit of measurement, in terms of his feet. The carpenter uses his own feet as the unit of measurement and the resulting bed is too small. The book provides an opportunity to discuss the problem of why the bed was too small before continuing the story. Have students share their ideas and understanding of the problem before continuing the story.

Finally, the problem of the bed is solved by sculpting a model of the king's foot to be used in all future measurements. Have students share their ideas about the possible problems with allowing each individual's foot to be used as a unit of measurement. Ask students if it would be a good idea to simply make the king do all the measurement. What problems would this create? Have students think about the sculpture of the king's foot. Is this the best solution? What difficulties might this present? What might be used instead of a sculpture?

Students may come up with the idea of some sort of ruler to take the place of the sculpture. Display a twelve-inch ruler. Explain that the ruler was invented to take care of the problems you have been discussing. Tell students that today things are measured in feet, which refers to the length of the ruler. Discuss the fact that the length of the ruler was originally based on the length of a king's foot, and that ruler is another name for a king.

Modeling

Explain to students that they will be measuring the length of various objects in the room with their own feet and also with the ruler, so that they can compare their feet to the king's foot.

Model measuring the length of an object using one of your own feet. Have students count with you to determine the length. Place the ruler beside your foot and ask whether it will take more or less of the king's feet (the ruler) to measure the length of the object. Ask students to justify their responses. Have them estimate how many of the ruler lengths it will take. Measure the object with the ruler and discuss the outcome.

Bring up the idea of measuring an object that is not on the floor (a window, for example). Draw out the idea that each student can create a ruler based on the size of his or her own feet. Show students the one-inch strips and explain that they may use them if they decide to measure things they cannot walk on or beside.

Action

Have students measure five objects in the room using their own feet. After each measurement, have them record their measurements and make estimates about how many of the king's feet, the ruler, it will take to cover the same distance. Then have them measure and record the distance.

Extensions

- Show students how to figure out the perimeter of the bed in the story and explore measuring perimeters of other objects.

- Have students explore the possibilities if the king had used his hand instead of his foot.

- Create a graph from the rulers students have made.

The King's Foot

Object	Length in My Feet	Estimate for the King's Feet	Length in the King's Feet

Body Perimeters

Strands

- Numeration
- Measurement
- Estimation

Materials

- Orange Cuisenaire® rods or tens rods (from Base Ten Blocks)
- Recording sheet

Description of Lesson

Overhead projector   yes ☐   no ☑

Conceptual Level	Concrete ☑	Connecting ☐	Abstract ☐
Instructional Level	Exposure ☑	Practice ☐	Mastery ☐

Purpose

To expose students to the ideas of perimeter and measurement with a standard unit of measure. To strengthen number relationships by estimating and by working with other rod lengths to develop the concept of proportionality (see Extensions).

Modeling

The language of perimeter should be introduced: "We are going to be measuring the perimeters of our bodies with orange rods. *Perimeter* means the distance around something. Would someone volunteer to be measured? Then I need someone else to draw an imaginary line around our volunteer to show us what is meant by the perimeter or distance around the outside of our body."

Once students understand what is meant by perimeter, ask a student to lie down on the floor and ask another student to come up and begin placing orange rods or tens rods around him or her to demonstrate how the rods will be used.

Action

Have students estimate the number of orange rods it would take to outline their bodies. Working with partners, students lie down while their partners begin outlining their bodies with orange rods. The student being outlined can help do the lower half of his or her body by sitting up. Once the orange rods are laid out, the student is helped up, and the rods are counted by tens and recorded. Have them reverse roles and repeat the process.

Discussion

Ask the class to predict which students will have the greatest perimeter and have them share their reasoning. Collect data from greatest to least perimeter distances on the board to verify the class's predictions.

Note: Some students may be sensitive regarding their height or body size, and care should be taken not to make them feel uncomfortable. Some alternatives are to

- choose five students of various sizes from other classes and grade levels. Before the lesson, trace their outlines on butcher paper, or on the sidewalk with chalk. Have your students predict which outline will have the greatest perimeter, which will have the least, and so on. Have them work in small groups to measure the outlines and check their estimates;

- have students predict your perimeter, instead of each other's;

- have students do only their arm or leg. This requires fewer rods, and can produce surprising results;

- have students measure objects other than bodies.

Extensions

- Repeat the lesson, asking the students to figure out their perimeters using yellow rods (half the length of orange rods). Many students who are familiar with rods and who have strong number relationships will realize that the number of rods needed for the perimeter will double. Others will need to do the activity, collect the data, and be guided to this discovery through class discussion. Ask if the distance has doubled or stayed the same (it is the number of units that has doubled, not the distance). This gives insight into students' abilities to conserve length and into their understanding of the role of units of measurement.

- You can repeat the lesson with other rods, or ask students merely to estimate what the actual number of rods would be using their prior information regarding their bodies' perimeters

- *The Line Up Book* (Russo 1986) provides an example of the use of nonstandard measures. In the book, Sam uses a variety of materials—blocks, toys, shoes, and books—to form a line from his bedroom to the kitchen. He is not measuring, but the idea of using objects to measure, and some techniques for measurement, can be brought out from the book. Students might then re-explore their perimeters using objects of their own choosing. Emphasis should continue to focus on estimating rather than measuring, and on making comparisons between different units of measure.

Body Perimeters

Color of Rod	Estimate	Actual
Orange		
Yellow		
Red		
White		
Green		

Average Height

Strands

- Measurement
- Numeration
- Number Operations
- Graphing/Statistics

Materials

- Links
- Calculator

Description of Lesson

Overhead projector   yes ☐   no ☑

Conceptual Level	Concrete ☑	Connecting ☐	Abstract ☐
Instructional Level	Exposure ☑	Practice ☐	Mastery ☐

Purpose

To expose students to the meaning of basic statistics terms *(range, mean/average, and median)* within the context of measurement. This lesson provides an excellent concrete model for understanding the concept and arithmetic process of averaging.

Action

Have students line up against the chalkboard, tallest to shortest. If they have trouble with this, appoint one student to arrange the class accordingly. Mark their heights on the chalkboard and have each student write his or her name under the corresponding mark.

Modeling

Teacher: "Which student is in the middle of our lineup?"

Student: "Josh."

Circle that student's name and mark and write the word *median* above the mark.

Action

Teacher: "That middle student is called the median of the group. There are an equal number of students on each side of him. What would happen to the median if the two tallest students were absent today?"

Student: "It would change."

Teacher: "How would it change? Can you come up and show me what the new median would be?"

The student comes up and finds the new median.

Teacher: "What seems to affect where the median is in our lineup?"

Student: "The number of people."

Teacher: "Would the median change if the tallest and shortest person were both absent?"

Student: "No, because you're just taking one off each end and the middle stays the same."

Student: "It's not the number of people exactly, it's how they are arranged."

Teacher: "We arranged our class from tallest to shortest. At one end we have Jamah and at the other end we have Sue. We say we have a range of heights from Jamah to Sue. If we change our range, the median might change or it might not. We've talked about one type of middle called the median. There is another type of middle that is called the *average*. Can anyone tell me what the word *average* means?"

Find out what the students know about averages and how they are used.

Teacher: "An average is what we would have if we were to make everything the same. Lets look at our heights. How could we make everyone the same height?"

Students may come up with various suggestions about stretching people, or they may feel that it is not possible.

Teacher: "You're right that we can't really do it, but if I could take some of Sue's height and give it to Jamah and take some of Charley's height and give it to Nanette and keep on doing that until everyone was the same height, everyone would be the average height. What would that look like when we lined everyone up then?"

Student: "A straight line."

Teacher: "We can't really share our heights, but we can make a model of our heights using links that would allow us to share."

Action

Have each students work with a partner to connect links into a chain that is equal to his or her height. Have students record the number of links in their chains under their names on the chalkboard.

Modeling

Model the sharing of heights (sharing links) by using two students to demonstrate in front of the class. Have them tell the class how many links long their chains are.

Teacher: "If Alex's chain is 48 links and Betsy's chain is 53 links, what could they do to share or average out their heights? They want to make both chains the same length."

Student: "Betsy should give Alex 5 links."

Student: "No, then Alex would have 53 and Betsy would have 48. The two chains wouldn't be equal. Betsy should give Alex 3 links."

Student: "But they still wouldn't be the same."

Teacher: "If Betsy gives Alex 3 links, how many links would each have?"

Have the two students share the links and tell how many they each have. In this case they have 50 and 51.

Teacher: "Is there any way that we can make it more even?"

Students will often suggest cutting the links in half. Have them agree to share links to get as close to even as possible without cutting links. Ask them to figure out some other sharing examples. Ask them what would happen if one student had 61 and another had 60.

Action

Have students find partners to average their links with. Once they have averaged with one person they should find someone else with whom to average. In a classroom of twenty-five students, it will take between three and five "sharings" to complete the averaging process.

Discussion

Check to make sure all averaging is complete by calling on students to tell the number of links in their chains. If all of the averaging has been completed, the class will have chains of only two different lengths (for example, 43 and 44). Compare the average height to the median height. The median and the average/mean will generally be very close for this project.

To make a connection with the arithmetic method for averaging, ask the class what would happen if you were to collect all the links in a bucket and then pass out the same number of links to each person. Most students will realize that they would have the same number of links that they currently hold.

Teacher: "How could we try this method without actually using the links and doing all that counting?"

Student: "Everyone's height is already on the board. If we add them all up, that would tell us how many links there are in the whole class."

Have the class work in groups to add up the total number of links. This would be a good time to use calculators. Once students have a sum, ask them how sharing is done mathematically—it is done by dividing. Have students divide the total number of links by the number of people in the class. The quotient should be the same as the number of links each student has. If the work was done on a calculator, the quotient will be expressed in decimal form, however.

Questions like the following may give insight into students' understanding of the arithmetic method of averaging: If we had everyone's height listed on the board in inches, what would we do to figure the average? If we had everyone's height listed in centimeters, what would we do to figure the average?

Ask students to come up with a general definition and rule for averaging and write it down on a piece of paper.

Extensions

■ Read *How Much Is a Million?* by David Schwartz, in which averages are used extensively.

■ Have students use the average of their heights to figure distances in terms of the number of average students laid end-to-end to reach a destination. For example, they might figure the number of average fourth graders laid end to end to go from New York to Los Angeles. These computations would involve figuring out how many average students in a mile and finding the distance in miles from various points. A project such as this can tie in with geography.

Making Numbers Make Sense

Tiles in Our Shoes

Strands

- Numeration
- Estimation
- Number Operations
- Measurement

Materials

- Tiles
- Construction paper
- Large grid for graphing

Description of Lesson

Overhead projector   yes ☐   no ☑

Conceptual Level	Concrete ☑	Connecting ☐	Abstract ☐
Instructional Level	Exposure ☑	Practice ☐	Mastery ☐

Purpose

To provide students with the opportunity to estimate, count, and add three-digit numbers using concrete materials.

Note: Students are not expected to know an algorithm for adding large numbers. Rather, they are invited to invent their own algorithms and are supported in doing so by the use of concrete materials and graphical representations. This lesson is most successful with students who are not yet aware that there exists a set way of doing such problems (an algorithm). Therefore, kindergartners and first graders may attack the problem with enthusiasm; whereas older students may be more hesitant and less willing to take risks.

Discussion

Ask students to think of some "math things" that they could do with shoes. It may be helpful to record their ideas for later investigations. It is important to validate students' contributions by allowing time for them to pursue some of their own ideas, either before this lesson or at a later time. If no one suggests it, tell them, "Today we are going to find out how many tiles our shoes will hold."

Modeling

Ask, "How many tiles do you think my shoe will hold?" Record students' estimates, then fill your shoe with tiles. Tell students, "Today you are going to fill your shoes with tiles and then count the tiles. When you count your tiles, I want you to organize them in a way that will make them easy to re-count. Once you have counted your tiles, I will ask you to raise your hand and I will come over and have you re-count them for me. Who can suggest a way that I might organize my tiles so that they will be easy to re-count?"

Students may suggest groupings of two, five, or ten depending upon their past experience in counting and grouping objects. Take some tiles from your shoe and begin silently counting and organizing the tiles according to the first suggested scheme. Ask, "How did I organize my tiles? Can someone show me how this makes them easy to re-count?" Have a student re-count the tiles. Repeat this procedure using schemes suggested by the students.

Assessment Note: Demonstrating a variety of ways to organize the tiles for counting validates students' own ideas and thinking. They will choose the scheme they are most comfortable with at this time. Move around the classroom and take notes on what types of groupings individuals are using. Students who do not choose to group by ten at this time may need more experience using the rote counting sequences of fives or tens or they may need additional opportunities to count, arrange, and manipulate smaller groups of objects.

Step 1: Explain to students that they will each fill up one of their shoes with tiles, empty it, group the tiles, and count them. Tell them to leave their tiles in the groups so that they can re-count them for you when you come around. While students are waiting for you, have them trace or draw a picture of their shoe, write the number of tiles they had on their picture, and cut out the shoe. The cutout shoes can be used for a graph in the extension.

Step 2: Have students begin filling their shoes with tiles at their work spaces. Once the shoes are filled, the tiles are grouped and counted. Students raise their hands to indicate that they are ready to re-count their tiles for you. As an alternative, you may want to have some students re-count their tiles for a partner, if you do not have time to get to all of them. Having students re-count for you provides an assessment of who knows the rote counting sequence. Many students do well up to 90 but need help continuing.

Step 3: Have students leave their grouped tiles at their work spaces and return to the floor with their cutout shoes. Select one student's paper shoe and place it on the floor so that everyone can see. Ask, "Who had a shoe that held more tiles than _____'s shoe? Who had a shoe that held fewer tiles than ____'s shoe?" Collect paper shoes from three students and ask the class to help you put the shoes in order from the least number of tiles to the greatest number of tiles. Repeat with other groups of three shoes.

Step 4: Have students form groups of three with the people who are working near them. In their group they will arrange their shoes in order from least to greatest and then figure out how many tiles they have used altogether to fill their three shoes. When they have figured out the total, have them paste their three shoes onto a large common sheet of newsprint and record the equation underneath (or you could record it for them).

▼ Extensions

- Form a class graph in which each square on the graph paper represents ten tiles. Rounding could be introduced in this context, and students could figure out the total number of tiles used by the whole class.

- All the students' paper shoes could be placed in order from least to greatest. Students could be called up to add their shoe to the proper place on the resulting number line.

- Ask students to further brainstorm and add to their list about mathematical things to be done with shoes. Allow them to pursue an individual or group investigation on their own.

Cover-Ups

Strands

- Numeration
- Estimation
- Measurement

Materials

- Recording sheet
- Small-portion cups
- Beans, one-centimeter cubes, or pennies
- Post-it™ notes

Description of Lesson

Overhead projector   yes ☑   no ☐

Conceptual Level	Concrete ☐	Connecting ☑	Abstract ☐
Instructional Level	Exposure ☐	Practice ☑	Mastery ☐

Purpose

To provide opportunities to make groups of tens and ones in counting. To explore area using a variety of materials.

Modeling

On the overhead projector, trace your hand. Ask the class to estimate how many beans it would take to cover the area of your hand, the space inside the lines. You may record the estimates, have students tell their estimates to their neighbors, or make an instant graph of the estimates using Post-it™ notes. To construct an instant graph or histogram, record a range of numbers for the expected estimates on the chalkboard (50–100 would be appropriate for this example). The numbers may be arranged vertically or horizontally and may progress by 1s, 2s, 5s, or 10s according to the available space. Give each student a Post-it™ note on which to write his or her name. Students then place their Post-it™ notes on the histogram to correspond to their estimates. Once this process is familiar to students, they can create a graph literally in an instant.

On the overhead projector, begin to fill in the area of your hand with the beans, starting with your fingers. Once all the fingers are filled in, tell the class that when they are counting the beans today you want them to place them in groups of ten. Model placing your beans in groups of ten, using a small-portion cup for each group of ten. Model counting the tens and then the ones with the class and recording the total. Ask them to reestimate now that they know how many beans it takes to fill the fingers, and have them justify their new estimates.

Action

Tell students to trace their hands on their recording sheets. Have them estimate how many beans, cubes, or pennies it will take to cover their hands, and have them record their estimates. Next, have them fill in their hands with either beans, cubes, or pennies, form groups of tens and ones (using the small-portion cups), and record their totals. Once students have finished their first investigations, have them repeat the procedure with a new material.

Discussion

Ask students to tell what they found out about the area of their hands in doing this. They will often mention that they found it takes less pennies than cubes and less cubes than beans to cover their hands. Probe further and ask them to explain why this is true.

▼ Extensions

- Use the book *3D, 2D, 1D* by David Adler to further explore the concept of area and the difference between linear and area measurement.

- Create a graph of "The Area of Our Hands in Beans." Discuss the range, median, and mode if appropriate. Ask the students if the graph would look the same if it were "The Area of Our Hands in Pennies" or "in Cubes."

- Repeat the activity using feet rather than hands.

The Area of My Hand

in Beans

Tens	Ones

in Cubes

Tens	Ones

in Pennies

Tens	Ones

Peter's Pockets

Strands

- Numeration
- Number Operations
- Measurement
- Graphing/Statistics

Materials

- *Peter's Pockets* by Eve Rice
- Unifix® cubes

Description of Lesson

Overhead projector   yes ☐   no ☑

Conceptual Level	Concrete ☑	Connecting ☐	Abstract ☐
Instructional Level	Exposure ☐	Practice ☑	Mastery ☐

Purpose

To promote an understanding of one-to-one correspondence, make comparisons between numbers, explore the special properties of zero in addition, and provide informal experiences in making number combinations using addition.

Discussion

Begin by reading the book *Peter's Pockets*, by Eve Rice. After reading the book turn back to the page that shows Peter's new pants, and have the class count the pockets. Explain to the class that they will be counting the number of pockets they have, to see if they have more or less pockets than Peter.

Action

Step 1: Demonstrate counting your pockets by placing one Unifix® Cube in each of your pockets. Have students place one Unifix® Cube in each of their pockets, using only one color of cube. Once all students have placed their Unifix® Cubes in their pockets, have them take them out and connect them into a train.

Step 2: Ask, "Raise your hand if you have more pockets than Peter." Call on students to state how many pockets they have. Ask, "Raise your hand if you have less pockets than Peter." Call on students to state how many pockets they have. Ask, "Has everyone raised his or her hand? Who hasn't raised his or her hand yet? Why haven't you raised your hand to one of my questions?" Draw out an understanding that some students may have the same number of pockets as Peter.

Modeling

Explain to the students that they will now form groups that have ten pockets altogether. Tell the students how many pockets you have, and show them your Unifix® Cube train. Ask, "Who in the class could come up here with me to make a total of ten pockets?" Call on a student to come up and tell the class how many pockets he or she has. Ask the class if together the two of you have ten pockets. Ask, "How might we check to make sure we have ten?" Combine the two Unifix® trains and count the cubes. Ask if there is any way to make ten pockets with three people. Model it for the class.

Step 3: Tell students to move around the room forming partnerships or small groups to make ten pockets. Some may not have any pockets. Take these students aside and tell them that they are special because they can combine with any group that already has ten. Point out to the class the special nature of zero in addition.

Discussion

Ask the class how they can figure out how many pockets there are in the whole class. Discuss their strategies and select one to carry out. As the cubes are already grouped by ten, this provides an easy way to count the total.

Extensions

- Keep track of the total number of pockets and repeat the counting of pockets on different days to make comparisons. Graph the results.

- Graph the total number of pockets for each table or group of students.

- For older students, figure out the average number of pockets each student has. Use the process of averaging described in the lesson "Average Height" to have students determine the average concretely.

Working with Physical Models

Weighing Pennies

Strands

- Measurement
- Numeration
- Estimation

Materials

- 300 – 400 pennies
- Jar
- 1 equal-arm balance for every 3 students (see directions, page 58)
- Recording sheet

Description of Lesson

Overhead projector   yes ☐   no ☑

Conceptual Level	Concrete ☐	Connecting ☑	Abstract ☐
Instructional Level	Exposure ☑	Practice ☐	Mastery ☐

Purpose

To provide students with a concrete experience using a balance to weigh objects. The concepts of equality, more, and less are developed informally in the lesson.

Discussion

To capture interest at the beginning of the lesson, place 300–400 pennies in a jar. Pass around the penny jar allowing each student to feel how heavy it is and estimate the number of pennies. Estimates may be shared verbally or by making an instant graph with Post-it™ notes (see "Cover-Ups" on page 50 for directions).

Action

Step 1: Have each student reach into the jar with eyes closed and grab what he or she thinks will be ten pennies. Have students count their actual number of pennies. Make an instant human histogram by having students seat themselves in rows of those who have eight pennies, nine, ten, eleven, and so on. Ask each row how many more pennies they need to make ten, or how many they need to give away. Give or take back the appropriate amounts.

Modeling

Ask the class if they think ten pennies will weigh more, less, or the same as a pencil. Demonstrate weighing the pencil using the equal-arm balance. Demonstrate recording the results on the recording sheet. Instruct students to weigh various objects, first predicting whether they will be lighter, heavier, or the same as their ten pennies. Recording may be done with pictures or writing.

Action

Step 2: Tell students to work with partners or in small groups to carry out investigations using their pennies. Have them find at least six objects that weigh about the same as ten pennies and record their findings on their recording sheets.

Extensions

- Repeat with 100 pennies.

- Have students check the accuracy of their earlier estimates by actually counting the pennies in the jar.

- Read *Who Sank the Boat?* by Pamela Allen. This is the story of a crew of animals who one-by-one climb aboard a small boat. The last one aboard is a mouse, who sinks the boat. The story uses a predictable pattern, making it accessible to young readers. The book allows students to discuss aspects of measuring, since sinking the boat is similar to tipping the balance.

Directions for Making an Equal-Arm Balance

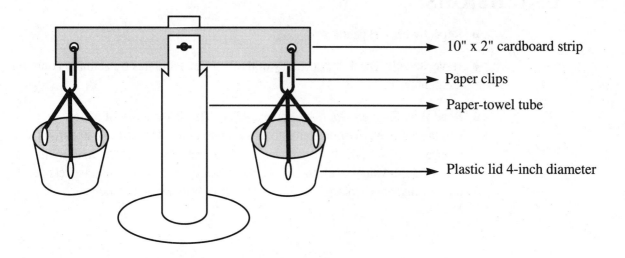

10" x 2" cardboard strip

Paper clips

Paper-towel tube

Plastic lid 4-inch diameter

Step 1: Cut a half-inch-wide by three-inch-long slit in both sides of the top of a paper-towel tube. Using a hole punch, punch holes a half inch from the top of both sides of the tube.

Step 2: Using a hot-glue gun, glue the paper-towel tube to the center of the plastic lid.

Step 3: Punch a hole one inch from each end of the cardboard strip, and one in the center.

Step 4: Assemble. Place the cardboard strip through the notched top of the cardboard tube, lining up the holes in the tube and the center of the strip. Straighten out one end of a large paper clip to go through the holes in the tube and center of the cardboard strip.

Step 5: Small, shallow plastic or paper cups work well to use as bowls for the balances. Punch three holes just below the rim of the bowl, spacing the holes equally around the circumference. Attach a piece of string about eight inches long to each hole. Gather the three strings together and tie them in a single knot. When the bowl is lifted by the knot, it should be balanced and not tilted (if the bowl is tilted,adjust the lengths of the strings).

Step 6: Attach a bowl to each side of the cardboard arm of the balance. Open a paper clip and attach one end underneath the knot and the other end through the endholes of the cardboard strip.

Hint: If the arm of the balance is uneven, a small piece of clay may be attached to the top of one side to make it even out.

Things That Weigh About 10 Pennies

1. _____

2. _____

3. _____

4. _____

5. _____

6. _____

on Paper

Strands

- Numeration
- Estimation

Materials

- Overhead transparency of recording sheet
- Recording sheet
- Crayons

Description of Lesson

Overhead projector   yes ☑   no ❏

Conceptual Level	Concrete ❏	Connecting ☑	Abstract ❏
Instructional Level	Exposure ☑	Practice ❏	Mastery ❏

Purpose

To provide practice counting and estimating and give experience grouping by ten.

Modeling

Show students the page of pennies on the overhead projector. Have them estimate how many pennies there are. Tell them they will write their estimates on their sheets and will count their pennies by coloring groups of ten pennies. Demonstrate coloring ten pennies with the same color on the overhead transparency. Switch to a different color for the next ten.

Action

Have students count and color groups of ten to figure out the actual number of pennies.

▼ Extensions

- Have students substitute dimes for each group of ten they have colored, then trade in ten dimes for a dollar.

- Read *The Hundred-Penny Box* by Sharon Bell Mathis. This is the story of a grandmother who collects a penny for each year of her life. For each penny, she tells her young grandson a memory attached to that year. At the end of the story the grandmother dies and the boy uses the hundred pennies to recall the memories that she shared.

Pennies on Paper

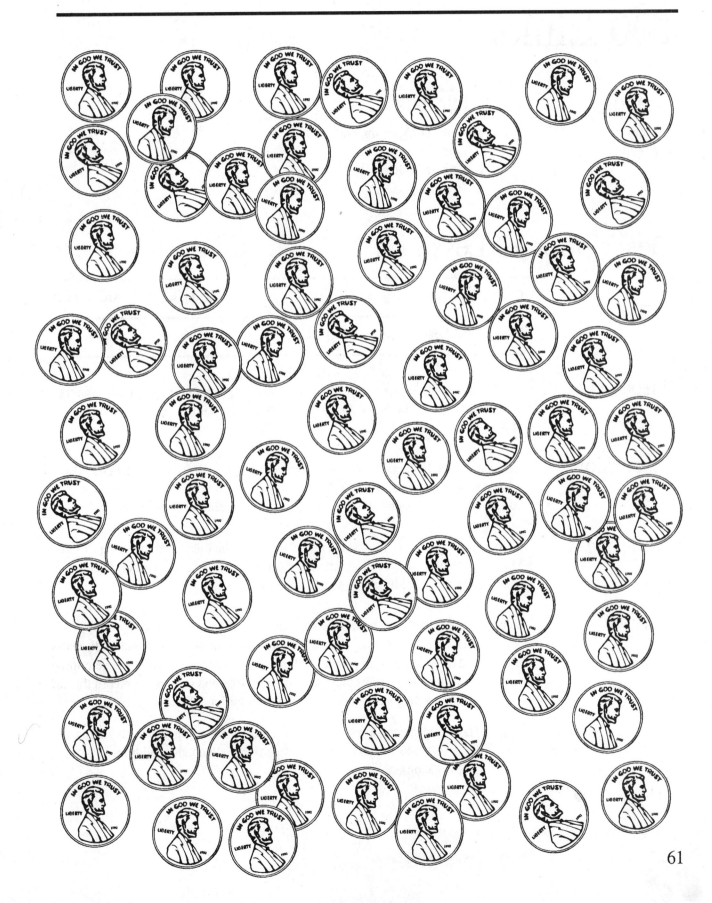

100 Links

Strands

- Measurement
- Numeration

Materials

- Links (100 per student)
- One sock per child
- Hundreds chart
- Recording sheet

Description of Lesson

Overhead projector   yes ☐   no ☑

Conceptual Level	Concrete ☑	Connecting ☐	Abstract ☐
Instructional Level	Exposure ☑	Practice ☐	Mastery ☐

Purpose

To provide counting experience, including practice grouping by tens and counting on (see the lesson "Handfuls" for information about counting on). To provide opportunities for measurement.

Discussion

Ask: Could you hold one hundred links in your hands? How many times do you think one hundred links will go around your waist? How far do you think one hundred links will reach? Will one hundred links be taller or shorter than you?

Modeling

Grab a double handful of links and model counting the links, making groups of 10. Mark your total on the hundreds chart and demonstrate how to count on to determine how many more links you would need to make 100.

Action

Step 1: Have students each grab a double handful of links and count them by making groups of 10. Have them mark their totals on their hundreds charts and on their recording sheets. Show students how to count on to determine how many more links they need to make 100, and have them record this on their recording sheets and count out the additional links they need.

Step 2: Have students answer the questions on their recording sheets and then use their 100 links to make further comparisons and conduct additional investigations.

▼ Extensions

- Link this lesson to other investigations of one hundred or to a celebration of the hundredth day of school.

- Create a class book of the things students found out about their hundred links. Each student can draw and label a picture showing his or her investigation. Other chapters may be added for investigations with a different collection of a hundred objects.

100 Links

_____ links fit into my hands.

I needed _____ more links to make 100.

100 links went around my waist _____ times.

I am *taller* *shorter* than 100 links (circle "taller" or "shorter").

Other things that I found out about 100 links:

_____

_____

_____

_____

_____

_____

_____

_____

Make a Dollar

Strands

- Measurement
- Numeration
- Number Operations
- Logic

Materials

- Play or real coins
- Coin stamps and ink pads
- Recording sheet
- *Dollars & Cents for Harriet* by Betsy and Giulio Maestro

Description of Lesson

Overhead projector   yes ☐   no ☑

Conceptual Level	Concrete ☐	Connecting ☑	Abstract ☐
Instructional Level	Exposure ☐	Practice ☑	Mastery ☐

Purpose

To provide experiences in working with money and establishing equivalency within a problem-solving context.

Preparation

Place one dollar of change in your pocket consisting of a variety of coins. For example: three quarters, two dimes, and five pennies.

Discussion

This lesson may be introduced by reading *Dollars & Cents for Harriet*. This book shows five different ways to form a dollar (representing the five dollars Harriet needs to buy a kite).

Review the value of all the coins with the class. Tell them that you have one dollar in coins in your pocket, and ask them to guess what you might have. Write the students' guesses on the chalkboard. Tell them that you will not say what you have until the end of the period when they have come up with all the possible combinations of coins.

Action

Have students work in groups to lay out and record combinations of coins that make a dollar. They may lay out a combination and ask a partner to check it before recording it. Students record their combinations on the "Make a Dollar" recording sheet by using the coin stamps that correspond to the coins they have laid out or by writing the coin values if stamps are not available.

Once students feel they have constructed all possible combinations, or they seem to be tiring, ask them how they could organize or sort their combinations. Students might suggest by the number of coins, by all the ones that use quarters, and so forth. Have the groups sort their combinations. Discuss any patterns or observations they have about combinations for a dollar.

Tell the class the number of coins you have in your pocket and have them guess the combination. Record on the chalkboard all the correct possibilities. Give additional clues until the class has discovered the combination you have.

▼ Extensions

- Chart all of the possibilities by the number of coins used and look for patterns. For example:

Number of Coins	Quarters	Dimes	Nickels	Pennies	Not Possible
100				100	✔
99					✔
98					✔
97					

- Students in third grade and up will be intrigued by other problems like the one in this lesson; for example, "I have ten coins that make a dollar and the coins are not all the same." Students enjoy making up their own riddles to challenge their classmates.

Make a Dollar

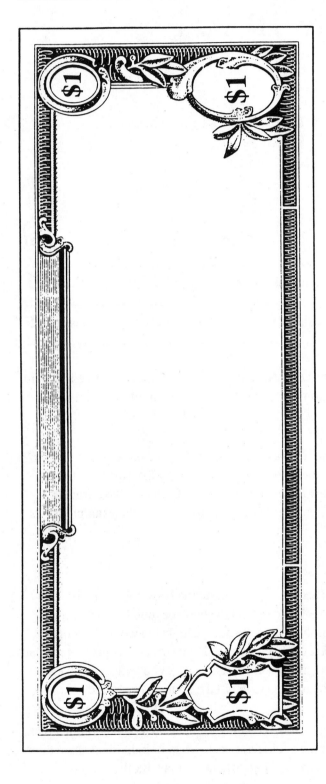

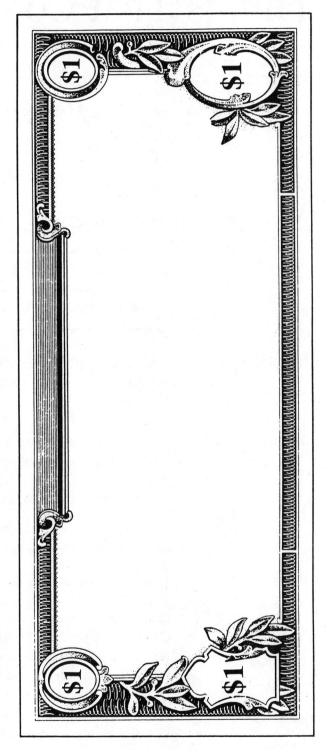

Things That Come In . . .

Strands

- Number Operations
- Numeration
- Measurement
- Patterns

Materials

- *What Comes in Two's, Three's & Four's* by Suzanne Aker

Description of Lesson

Overhead projector   yes ☐   no ☑

Conceptual Level	Concrete ☐	Connecting ☐	Abstract ☑
Instructional Level	Exposure ☑	Practice ☐	Mastery ☐

Purpose

To examine everyday objects and events from a mathematical perspective in regard to their grouping and organization. To begin exploration of multiplication within this context.

Discussion

Show students the cover of *What Comes in Two's, Three's & Four's?* Ask them to think of things that naturally come in 2s or are organized by 2s. Record students' responses. Share some of the examples from the book if students have trouble getting started. After they have run out of ideas, share some of the examples of 2s from the book.

Repeat this procedure for 3s and 4s.

Have students share their ideas about why they think the book ends with 4s. Discuss whether it would be possible to extend the book beyond 4s. Ask which numbers would be easy to incorporate into the book and which would be more difficult. Ask how high the book could be extended. Have students generate a plan for extending the book: What numbers will be included? Who will work on each number? What materials will be used? How will the book be organized?

Action

Have students work to extend the book according to the class's predetermined plan. Before assembling the pages of the book, have each group or individual share their pages with the class. Students experiencing difficulties may ask the class for additional ideas for their pages.

▼ Extensions

- Post a list of the items students have generated for each number. Use this list to generate multiplication problems: If you had three tables, how many legs would there be? How many sides are there on four stop signs?

- Explore multiples of objects. Have students pick an object from their list and draw a picture of it, then two pictures of the object, then three, and so on. Beside each picture, students record the multiplication equations that match their drawings. For example, beside a picture of three tables a student would write $3 \times 4 = 12$.

Build a Number

Strands

- Numeration
- Estimation

Materials

- Envelopes (one per student)
- Three-by-five-inch index cards (one per student)
- Base Ten Blocks
- Recording Sheet

Description of Lesson

Overhead projector   yes ☑   no ☐

Conceptual Level	Concrete ☐	Connecting ☑	Abstract ☐
Instructional Level	Exposure ☐	Practice ☑	Mastery ☐

Purpose

To reacquaint students with Base Ten Blocks and to reinforce place-value concepts through work with concrete objects. To reinforce counting on by hundreds, tens, and ones.

Preparation

Write a different letter of the alphabet on each envelope. After "Z," move to "AA," "BB," and so on. On each index card write a number. The magnitude of the numbers should match the students' ability but should not exceed 999 unless thousands cubes are available. Place each card in an envelope, keeping a record of the number corresponding to each letter (for example, A = 54, B = 897).

Base Ten Blocks may be used for demonstrating on the overhead projector, or you may make overhead base ten blocks from plastic netting. The netting forms a transparent grid so the tens and hundreds can actually be counted when viewed on the overhead projector (regular Base Ten Blocks only appear as solid shadows). Also, grids made from netting will be much smaller than Base Ten Blocks, so you can fit more on the screen. Purchase the plastic netting from a craft store and cut it into 10 x 10 squares for the hundreds, 1 x 10 rectangles for the tens, and 1 x 1 squares for the ones.

Modeling

Review the Base Ten Blocks with the students by saying, "If this cube is 1, how many of these would it take to make this rod? How many of these little 1s cubes would it take to make this large square?"

Place some Base Ten Blocks on the overhead projector and ask "If I were to trade these all in for 1s cubes, how many would this arrangement be worth?" Have several students explain how they counted the blocks.

Action

Step 1: Give each student a secret number in an envelope. Their job is to build a structure that represents the number using Base Ten Blocks. The structure may lay flat or be built up, but all the blocks used must be visible. It is often best to allow students to spread out so that they feel they have more privacy. Also, structures built on the floor are less likely to get bumped and topple over.

Step 2: After all students have finished building, tell them to place their secret number back in the envelope and leave it letter-side-up beside their structure. Have them estimate and then actually count the numbers that their classmates' buildings represent, recording building A's estimate and count on line A, and so on.

Discussion

Discuss with students their techniques for making an estimate and for actually counting the blocks in each building. Have them identify the range of numbers that were represented. Have students read off their actual numbers for the structures they built.

Extensions

- Have students graph the numbers and identify the range and median.

- Have the class estimate the total number of blocks used for all the buildings combined. Since the concrete materials are available, this problem would be accessible even to second graders given adequate time. Ask students to suggest strategies and then carry out one strategy for the whole class. For example, they will often suggest bringing all the blocks to a central location, sorting them, and then counting. Once students have counted, facilitate by asking them to make trades. For example, if students have counted 23 tens, ask, "Could we trade these 23 tens for some hundreds squares?"

Build a Number

Estimate	Actual	Estimate	Actual
A. _____	A. _____	U. _____	U. _____
B. _____	B. _____	V. _____	V. _____
C. _____	C. _____	W. _____	W. _____
D. _____	D. _____	X. _____	X. _____
E. _____	E. _____	Y. _____	Y. _____
F. _____	F. _____	Z. _____	Z. _____
G. _____	G. _____	AA. _____	AA. _____
H. _____	H. _____	BB. _____	BB. _____
I. _____	I. _____	CC. _____	CC. _____
J. _____	J. _____	DD. _____	DD. _____
K. _____	K. _____	EE. _____	EE. _____
L. _____	L. _____	FF. _____	FF. _____
M. _____	M. _____	GG. _____	GG. _____
N. _____	N. _____	HH. _____	HH. _____
O. _____	O. _____	II. _____	II. _____
P. _____	P. _____	JJ. _____	JJ. _____
Q. _____	Q. _____	KK. _____	KK. _____
R. _____	R. _____	LL. _____	LL. _____
S. _____	S. _____	MM. _____	MM. _____
T. _____	T. _____	NN. _____	NN. _____

Measuring with Pennies

Strands

- Numeration
- Measurement
- Estimation
- Number Operations
- Algebra
- Patterns

Materials

- 1,000–2,000 pennies
- Recording sheets

Description of Lesson

Overhead projector   yes ☐   no ☑

Conceptual Level	Concrete ☐	Connecting ☑	Abstract ☐
Instructional Level	Exposure ☑	Practice ☐	Mastery ☐

Purpose

To provide students with an opportunity to explore various aspects of linear measurement using nonstandard measures (pennies) and discover the formulas for perimeter and area.

Discussion

Hold up a book and ask students what things about the book might be measured. They might suggest the length of sides, perimeter, diagonals, area, number of pages, thickness, and so forth. Standard terms may be introduced as the concepts come up, for example, the word perimeter may be introduced when a student suggests measuring the distance around.

Tell the class that they will be measuring with pennies, and ask what things about the book might be measured with pennies. Review the definitions of perimeter and diagonal if needed.

Modeling

Tell the class that they will select flat rectangular objects (such as books, tabletops, or paper) to measure using pennies. Model measuring and recording the sides of a book with pennies, and ask the class how you should measure the area or space enclosed by the sides of the book. Demonstrate covering the book with pennies and filling in as much space as possible.

Action   Have students work with partners to measure an object and fill out the recording sheet. While making their estimates, they may recognize the relationship between the sides and the perimeter and area.

Discussion   Discuss any strategies that students developed for estimating perimeter and area. A formula may evolve from this discussion.

Extensions

- Give students various dimensions for a rectangular object's sides, and ask them to figure out the area and perimeter.

- Use the book *3D, 2D, 1D* by David Adler to further explore the concept of area and the difference between linear and area measurement.

Names _____

Measuring with Pennies

What we measured: _____

	Estimate	Actual
Side	_____	_____
Side	_____	_____
Perimeter (the distance around the outside)	_____	_____
Area (the space fenced in by the sides)	_____	_____
Diagonal	_____	_____

Dimes and Pennies

Strands

- Numeration
- Logic
- Number Operations
- Measurement

Materials

- Overhead coins
- Dice, dimes, and pennies
- Recording sheet

Description of Lesson

Overhead projector   yes ☑   no ☐

Conceptual Level	Concrete ☑	Connecting ☐	Abstract ☐
Instructional Level	Exposure ☐	Practice ☑	Mastery ☐

Purpose

To deepen understanding of place value, particularly of tens and ones, using money as a context in a problem-solving game.

Note

Overhead coins may be made by making a photocopy of coin stamps and then producing a transparency from the photocopy.

Modeling

Model the game on the overhead projector.

Object of Game: To come closer than your opponent to one dollar, without going over, after seven rolls of the die.

Rules: Player 1 rolls the die and selects whether to take that number as pennies or dimes. He or she places the pennies or dimes on the first line of the recording sheet.

Player 2 then rolls the die and selects whether to take that number as pennies or dimes, placing them on his or her recording sheet.

Play continues until each player has taken seven turns or until one player goes over one dollar.

Players add their coins, trading for dimes when they need to do so. The player closest to one dollar without going over is the winner.

▼ Extensions

- The game may be played with Base Ten Blocks. Rather than taking the number as dimes or pennies, the students choose to take either tens rods or ones cubes. The object is to come as close to 100 as possible.

- The game may be played symbolically. Students label their columns "Tens" and "Ones." They choose to write their roll in the Tens column or in the Ones column. At the end of seven rolls they add to see who is closer to 100.

- The game may be played as a subtraction game. Each player starts with a dollar, a hundreds square, or 100 (symbolically). Depending on the materials being used, the player selects to subtract either a dime or penny, a tens rod or ones cube, or 10 or 1. The player closest to zero wins.

Dimes and Pennies

	Dimes	Pennies
1.		
2.		
3.		
4.		
5.		
6.		
7.		
TOTAL		

Coin Combos

Strands

- Numeration
- Number Operations
- Logic
- Patterns

Materials

- 1,000–2,000 pennies (real or play)
- Recording sheets
- Other money denominations are optional

Description of Lesson

Overhead projector   yes ☑   no ☐

Conceptual Level	Concrete ☐	Connecting ☑	Abstract ☐
Instructional Level	Exposure ☐	Practice ☑	Mastery ☐

Purpose

To expose students to writing dollar amounts using a decimal point, and to reinforce an understanding of the value of each coin. To provide work with addition and substitution using coin values.

Discussion

Asks a student in the class to estimate the number of pennies you would be able to hold in a double handful of pennies. On the overhead recording sheet, record the student's estimate, for example, 217.

Teacher: "If I take these 217 pennies to the bank, how many dollar bills would they give me?"

Student: "Two."

Teacher: "Why two?"

Student: "Because it takes 100 pennies for a dollar, and you have 200 pennies, so you would get 2 dollars."

Record the 2 on the recording sheet.

Teacher: "Would there be any pennies left over after I traded the 200 pennies for 2 dollars?"

Student: "Yes, 17 pennies."

Record the 17 pennies on the recording sheet. Demonstrate how to write $2.17, explaining that the number before the decimal point refers to the dollars and the number after the decimal point refers to the number of cents, or pennies.

Teacher: "Instead of giving me back two dollars and seventeen pennies for my 217 pennies, are there any other combinations that the bank teller might give me?"

Note the students' suggested combinations on the recording sheet. For example:

Dollars	Quarters	Dimes	Nickels	Pennies
2		1	1	2
	8		3	2

Action

Have the class form workgroups. Have students each grab a handful of pennies and count them. They then figure out the total number of pennies they have in their group and use this total to complete their recording sheets.

The pennies may be collected after counting. Play nickels, dimes, and quarters may be used to model the coin exchanges concretely if needed.

▼ Extensions

- Ask the class to imagine they are training people to work at a bank. At the bank they always give people the fewest number of coins possible when exchanging money. Have students devise a simple rule or procedure that could be explained to new bank tellers to enable them to give back the least number of coins for each exchange.

- *26 Letters and 99 Cents* by Tana Hoban displays a variety of coin combinations for different amounts of money. *Dollars & Cents for Harriet* by Betsy and Giulio Maestro shows five different ways to form a dollar. After having a chance to look at these books, students might use rubber coin stamps to create a book of their own, showing, for example, all the ways to make $2.17.

© Addison-Wesley Publishing Company, Inc.

Name _____

Coin Combos

Number of Pennies: _____

How many dollar bills could you trade for? ☐   Pennies left over? ⬭

We can write that amount as $ ☐ • ⬭

Dollars	Quarters	Dimes	Nickels	Pennies

Grains of Rice

Strands

- Estimation
- Numeration
- Number Operations
- Measurement
- Patterns

Materials

- Bucket
- 10 –15 pounds of rice (dyed rice is preferable)
- An assortment of the following:
  Equal-arm balance and 1-pound weights (see the lesson "Weighing Pennies" for directions on how to make an equal-arm balance
- Small cups for counting
- Measuring spoons
- Measuring cups

Description of Lesson

Overhead projector   yes ☐   no ☑

Conceptual Level	Concrete ☐	Connecting ☑	Abstract ☐
Instructional Level	Exposure ☐	Practice ☑	Mastery ☐

Purpose

To give students the opportunity to practice their estimating skills and devise strategies for estimating large quantities. Prior experience estimating and counting is needed to be successful with this lesson.

Action

Display the bucket of rice. Have students work in small groups to devise and write plans for figuring out how many grains of rice there are in the container (12 pounds of rice will be approximately 250,000 grains of rice). You may want to display a variety of measuring spoons, cups, and the balance to help students think of way to organize the rice for counting.

Discussion

Ask: What makes one method better than another for determining the number of grains of rice? Establish criteria for judging strategies: accuracy, speed, fun. Chart five or six of the students' strategies. Include counting the rice as a strategy, if students have not, to show that counting would be accurate but very slow. Rate the strategies in terms of accuracy and speed; for example, the most accurate strategy gets a "1," the next most accurate a "2," and so on. Use the chart to evaluate the strategies.

Modeling

Depending on the background knowledge and skill of the students, it may be necessary to model the techniques for estimating the rice. The group of students whose strategy is being used can help with the modeling. For example, one strategy might be to count a tablespoon of rice and then figure out how many tablespoons are in the entire bucket (a tablespoon will hold approximately two hundred grains of rice). While it is possible to figure the number of tablespoons in the bucket, it may be preferable to figure the number of tablespoons in a cup and then the number of cups in the bucket. In this way, more students may be involved in the process. In addition, when they come up with differing amounts for a tablespoon, averages may be discussed.

Action

Have the class select a few strategies to actually carry out. Compare results from different strategies, asking what accounts for the differences, and which one is a closer approximation.

Procedure for Dying Rice

Students can dye the rice or you can do it beforehand. In a one-gallon storage bag, pour 1/4 cup of rubbing alcohol. Add 15–30 drops of food coloring. Add two cups of rice, seal the bag, and shake until the rice is thoroughly coated. More food coloring may be added to darken the color if desired. If excess liquid remains in the bag, add additional rice. Spread the rice out on newspaper to dry, which will take about two hours. The smell of rubbing alcohol can be quite strong while the rice is drying. Plan to dry the rice at the end of the day or in a location where the odor will not affect students.

Extensions

- Read *The King's Chessboard* by David Birch or *A Grain of Rice* by Helena Pittman. Both books detail what happens when an initial quantity (in this case one grain of rice) is continually doubled over time. This exponential growth is fascinating for students and both stories put the procedure in an interesting context that will further capture students' attention.

- After introducing *The King's Chessboard*, ask students to figure out the day on which the Wise Man in the story will receive one pound of rice. Students can use what they have learned in the lesson to help them.

- Have students check the computations of the Weigher in *The King's Chessboard*, particularly the number of grains of rice in one dry ounce.

The Richter Scale

Strands

- Numeration
- Number Operations
- Measurement
- Graphing/Statistics
- Algebra
- Patterns

Materials

- Cuisenaire® rods
- Color Tiles
- Wooden cubes
- Base Ten Blocks

Description of Lesson

Overhead projector   yes ☐   no ☑

Conceptual Level	Concrete ☑	Connecting ☐	Abstract ☐
Instructional Level	Exposure ☑	Practice ☐	Mastery ☐

Purpose

To provide a concrete model of exponential growth as it relates to the Richter scale.

Discussion

Engage the class in a discussion about what they know about earthquakes. If the students do not bring up the Richter scale, mention it to see what they know. Tell the class that they will be building cities from blocks, and that when they are finished you will simulate earthquakes to learn more about the Richter scale.

Action

Have students work in small groups to build cities from Cuisenaire® rods, Color Tiles, and wooden cubes. These should be built on table tops, leaving adequate room around each city to drop the blocks that will be used later to simulate the intensities of various earthquakes (leave about one square foot of space). Allow about fifteen minutes for students to build their cities.

Discussion

Tell the class that you will be simulating the strength of various earthquakes measured by the Richter scale. Explain that each subsequent number on the Richter scale represents a tenfold increase in the intensity of the earthquake, and that you will be dropping a one-centimeter cube to simulate a 1 on the Richter scale. Ask them what would represent a 2 on the scale (a tens rod), a 3 on the scale (a hundreds square), a 4 on the scale (a thousands cube), and a 5 on the scale (ten thousands cubes). Ask the class to predict what will happen after each block is dropped, and what destruction will occur.

Modeling

From a height of about two feet drop a one-centimeter square cube onto the table about a foot away from one of the cities. Notice the effect on the city; it should be nothing. Explain that this is equivalent to an earthquake registering 1 on the Richter scale. A 1 is usually not felt. Drop a tens rod from the same height and notice the effect. This is equivalent to a 2 on the scale and is the lowest level usually felt by humans but which causes no damage to buildings. Drop a hundreds square for a 3, a thousands cube for a 4, and ten thousands cubes (at once) for a 5. A 4 or a 5 will probably wipe out the cities, due to their weak foundations. In real life a 7 or 8 could produce this much damage.

Decimals may also be introduced in the context of the Richter scale. If we use a hundreds square to represent a 3 on the scale, what would five hundreds squares represent? (a 3.5).

Discussion

Discuss the results and what was realistic and unrealistic about this simulation: for example, earthquakes happen from below rather than above and occur in waves, and buildings have foundations that make them more stable. Discuss what a 6, 7, and 8 on the Richter scale would be like in this model. Write the numbers 1, 10, 100, 1000, and so forth on the chalkboard and discuss a logarithmic scale and exponential growth.

 # Extensions

- Have students graph the exponential growth of the Richter scale.

- *Powers of Ten* by Morrison and Eames is both a book and a film that dramatically demonstrates exponential growth and a logarithmic scale similar to the Richter Scale. Starting with a picture taken from a distance of one meter (of a man having a picnic), the image is gradually changed as the frame of the picture is moved to ten meters away, then one hundred meters away, and so on through the galaxies to an eventual distance of one billion light-years. Then the original scene shown from one meter is shown from a distance of 10 centimeters, then 1 centimeter, and so on to a microscopic level. While the images are accessible to all students, the text is beyond the comprehension of most elementary students.

- With older students, use the "Exploring the Mathematics of the Richter Scale" sheet to probe further into logarithms.

Exploring the Mathematics of the Richter Scale

In the normal counting sequence we have a scale of one. This means that each number is one bigger than the previous number—for any two consecutive numbers in the counting sequence, the difference between the numbers is one. In a common logarithmic scale (meaning the scale is built on base ten) such as the Richter scale, this is not the case. Each number on the scale is ten times the previous one. This means that the scale between numbers is not constant. For example, in the Richter scale the difference between a 1 and a 2 is slight. Using our model, the numerical difference between a ones cube and a tens stick is nine units. However, the difference between a 4 and a 5 on the Richter scale is substantial. This can be seen in our model: the difference between one thousand and ten thousand is nine thousand. In a logarithmic scale, this dramatic increase in the growth of the magnitude of sequential numbers is said to be exponential or geometric.

The base ten logarithm or common log of a number indicates the power or exponent to which 10 must be raised to obtain the number. For example, to find the log of 100 you ask, "What power of 10 equals 100?" 10^2 (ten to the second power, or 10×10) equals 100. The log of 100 is then 2 since 10 must be raised to the second power to reach 100. Working backwards, a 5 on the Richter scale (or any common logarithmic scale) means 10^5, or 100,000.

You can see this connection by writing the logarithmic scale above the numbers they represent. Complete the chart below (use a separate sheet of paper if you need more room):

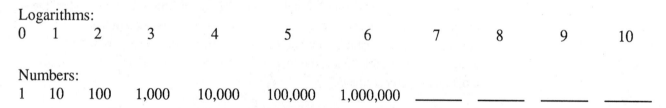

Logarithms:
0   1   2   3   4   5   6   7   8   9   10

Numbers:
1   10   100   1,000   10,000   100,000   1,000,000   _____   _____   _____   _____

What pattern do you see in the number of zeros in the number and the logarithm? Each of these numbers can be written as a product of 10s. For example, $1,000 = 10 \times 10 \times 10$. This can also be written as a power of 10, 10^3. Write each of the numbers above as a power of ten.

A Million Blades of Grass

Strands

- Numeration
- Estimation
- Number Operations

Materials

- Recording sheet
- Grass
- Butter knives
- Color Tiles
- Toothpicks
- Calculators

Description of Lesson

Overhead projector   yes ☐   no ☑

Conceptual Level	Concrete ☐	Connecting ☐	Abstract ☑
Instructional Level	Exposure ☐	Practice ☑	Mastery ☐

Purpose

To give students the opportunity to work with large numbers while employing addition and multiplication skills in an interesting context.

Discussion

Ask the students, "If you had to buy grass by the blade for a lawn, how many blades of grass do you think you would need? How many for our playground (or for a nearby park)? Would a million blades of grass be enough? Is there any way we could figure out the area a million blades would cover?" Guide them to the idea of taking a small sample and counting the blades of grass in it.

Action

Have students use their recording sheets to make estimates and follow one of the two procedures listed. The procedures may need to be modeled depending on the ages of the students. As an alternative to the independent nature of the recording sheet, dig up one square foot of grass, or purchase a roll of sod, and have it in the classroom. Students can take their samples from the precut sod without flipping a tile.

Sod can be difficult to cut. You may want to divide up a square foot of sod among students and add their results to figure the total number of blades in the square foot. Calculators may be used to compute the number of square inches or feet needed for a million.

Extensions

- Ask students to investigate different types of grass to determine the density of each, or have them figure out the approximate cost of a square foot of grass grown from seed.

- Have students determine the number of blades of grass on the playground or in a nearby park.

- *How Much Is a Million,* by David Schwartz, presents many representations of millions, billions, and trillions. Students may add their own representations of a million to a class book starting with the information they have found out in this lesson.

A Million Blades of Grass

How many blades of grass do you think are in one square inch of lawn?

Estimate:_____ Actual:_____

How many square inches of lawn do you think it will take to make
1,000,000 blades of grass?

Estimate: _____ Actual: _____

Find out from your teacher whether you will be using Procedure #1 or
Procedure #2 below.

Procedure 1:

1. Take a Color Tile outside and flip it in the air. This is so you will select a
   random section of grass.

2. With a knife cut around the outside of the Color Tile. You will need to cut
   1–2 inches deep. Pull up your grass square and bring it inside.

3. Use a toothpick to help you separate and count the blades of grass.

4. Use this information to figure out approximately how many square inches
   of grass it would take to make a million blades of grass.

Procedure 2:

1. Carefully cut out the square inch below so there is a hole in your paper.

2. Drop this page on the grass.

3. Use a toothpick to help you separate and count the blades of grass
   showing through the square hole.

4. Use this information fo figure out approximately how many square inches
   of grass it would take to make a million blades of grass.

Abstracting
and Extending

A Dollar's Worth

Strands

- Number Operations
- Measurement
- Numeration
- Estimation
- Algebra
- Patterns

Materials

- *The Go-Around Dollar* by Barbara Adams
- *Money* by Joe Cribb
- *The One Dollar Word Riddle Book* by Marilyn Burns
- *Alexander, Who Used to Be Rich Last Sunday* by Judith Viorst
- *If You Made a Million* by David Schwartz

Description of Lesson

Overhead projector　　yes ☐　　no ☑

Conceptual Level	Concrete ☐	Connecting ☐	Abstract ☑
Instructional Level	Exposure ☐	Practice ☑	Mastery ☐

Purpose

To provide the opportunity for students to take responsibility for their own learning by choosing to explore an aspect of money. What students learn will be determined by their choice of an investigation.

Discussion

Share briefly what each of the five books is about. A synopsis of each one follows:

The Go-Around Dollar follows the life of a dollar from person to person. Along the way, interesting facts about the design and construction of dollar bills are revealed.

Money, a book in the Eyewitness series, examines money from around the world. It includes the history of money and how it is produced.

The One Dollar Word Riddle Book presents a scheme in which each letter of the alphabet is assigned a value, A = 1¢, B = 2¢, C = 3¢, and so on. Students try to come up with words whose additive values equal one dollar and complete the riddles.

Alexander, Who Used to Be Rich Last Sunday follows Alexander as he progressively spends and loses the dollar his grandparents gave him.

If You Made a Million explores the effects of compound interest on money over time while presenting interesting physical models of various amounts of money.

Tell the students they will have an opportunity to examine and read the books and will be asked to choose one book to explore or extend in some way. If you have multiple copies of these books then this will be easier. If not, allow several days to give students an opportunity to look at the books.

Modeling

If students are not used to working independently on projects of their own choosing, you may need to model what their investigation may look like. For example, after reading *If You Made a Million,* a student might explore compound interest further by finding out what current interest rates are and refiguring some of the amounts presented in the book. After reading *Money,* students might explore current values of foreign currency. The amounts in *Alexander* may seem dated to students and they might rewrite the book with current prices. You could facilitate this by having the class brainstorm about the things that might be done with each book. List the ideas and have students choose from the list.

Action

Students may work independently or in small groups to carry out their investigations. Some students may require more time than others depending on their investigations. Set a date for the sharing of students' investigations and give them time daily to work. This will allow you to check in with each group and monitor its progress.

Discussion

Have students share their findings with their classmates. This may be done in small groups or as a whole class. Students might visit other classes to share what they found out. Students need to know that their contributions are valued. This provides the motivation for their learning.

Extensions

- Create a bulletin board display to show what students have learned about money.

- Visit a local bank to find out more about how they work and the services they offer.

- Have students design their own dollar bill.

Newspaper Numbers

Strands

- Numeration

Materials

- Newspapers or magazines
- Cash register tape

Description of Lesson

Overhead projector   yes ☐   no ☑

Conceptual Level	Concrete ☐	Connecting ☐	Abstract ☑
Instructional Level	Exposure ☑	Practice ☐	Mastery ☐

Purpose

To provide students with a visual model of the relative magnitude of numbers.

Note

This lesson can be done individually or as a whole-class project. The background of the students involved will dictate the degree of accuracy expected. Some knowledge of scale and fractional parts is helpful.

Action

Have students cut out numbers they find in newspapers or magazines. This can be done in class or at home.

Modeling

Roll out a length of cash register tape, approximately ten feet. Have students sit in a half-circle around the tape so that they can see. Mark zero on the left end, and have students come and place their numbers where they think they should go on the number line.

Discussion

Discussion should arise as students place new numbers on the line. The need for a scale should emerge. Highlight this by giving various examples: "If I placed 100 here, where would I put 200? 500? 1,000? If this is where we put one million, where would we put half a million? How does 100,000 relate to a million?" Large numbers should be discussed within the context in which they were found. For example, "Jessica, when you found 1.2 billion in the newspaper, what was being described?"

With very large numbers, maintaining the appropriate scale becomes impractical. For example, to properly place 1,000,000 on the number line would require repeating the distance from 0 to 1,000 a thousand times. With upper elementary and middle school students you will want to explore this concept of scale. With younger students, ordering numbers appropriately should be the emphasis.

Extensions

- This can be a permanent classroom display that is added to on a regular basis. More tape can be added to the number line.

- Students can explore newspapers further through the book *How Newspapers Are Made* by Walters.

Daily Numbers

Strands

- Numeration
- Estimation

Materials

- The day's newspaper

Description of Lesson

Overhead projector   yes ☐   no ☑

Conceptual Level	Concrete ☐	Connecting ☐	Abstract ☑
Instructional Level	Exposure ☐	Practice ☑	Mastery ☐

Purpose

To develop students' number sense through the examination of numbers in context.

Preparation

Look through the day's newspaper to find approximately five instances of numbers being used in context. Try to have a variety of numbers that differ in magnitude. Record the sentences on the chalkboard (or on an overhead transparency), leaving a blank space where the numbers belong. In a separate section on the chalkboard, record the numbers in a random order.

SENTENCES FROM TODAY'S NEWSPAPER	NUMBERS
Apparent winners of both the women's _____ kilometer race walk and the men's _____ meter run were disqualified, leading to gold medals by Chen Yueling of China in the walk and to Richard Chemlimo, _____, from Kenya.	234 49,279 19
In the new school board proposal, another _____ new classrooms would be added to existing schools.	10,000
Each of the proposals must be backed by at least _____ valid signatures of legally registered voters.	10

Discussion

Example:
Explain to students that you have copied several sentences that contain numbers from the day's newspaper but you have left the numbers out. Share the sentences with the students and encourage them to speculate on the numbers that are missing. Ask students to explain their reasoning.

Action

Show students the numbers that need to go in the blanks. Have them work in small groups or with partners to discuss where the numbers should go. Allow a few minutes for discussion, and then call on individuals to share and justify their group's predictions. Allow other groups to disagree. Reveal the correct placement of each number. You may wish to show students the articles from which the sentences came to encourage independent reading.

Extensions

- Use this activity as a daily opening for the class.

- Have students create their own Daily Numbers exercises.

- Students can find out more about how a daily newspaper is produced through the book *Hot Off the Press* by Crismann.

Place-Value Graphing

Strands

- Numeration
- Estimation
- Graphing/Statistics
- Logic

Materials

- Containers of precounted items (straws, paper clips, beans, or Color Tiles)
- Overhead transparency of the recording sheet

Description of Lesson

Overhead projector   yes ☑   no ☐

Conceptual Level	Concrete ☐	Connecting ☐	Abstract ☑
Instructional Level	Exposure ☐	Practice ☑	Mastery ☐

Purpose

To reinforce place-value understanding of hundreds, tens, and ones within the context of estimation.

Discussion

Discuss with students that the purpose of estimating is not to get the exact answer but a reasonable approximation. Tell them that one way to judge the reasonableness of an estimate is to look at how many places (hundreds, tens, or ones) are correct. For example, if the actual quantity of beans is 247, an estimate of 256 would have one place correct—the hundreds. An estimate of 243 would have two places correct—the hundreds and the tens. An estimate of 247 would have all three places correct. For this activity, the places are considered correct only if all previous places are correct. Thus, we will say that the tens place is correct only if the hundreds place is also correct, and the ones place is correct only if the hundreds and tens places are also correct. Using the above example, we would say the estimate 347 has no places correct. An estimate of 251 is closer to the actual number than an estimate of 241, but it only has one place correct. This lesson emphasizes looking at place value rather than focusing on which estimate is closer.

When students estimate actual quantities, their estimates usually contain a digit other than zero in each place. This is in contrast to computational estimation, which stresses rounding off numbers.

Action

Show students a container of straws and ask them to estimate how many there are. Record the estimates either on the chalkboard or along the edge of an overhead transparency for use in constructing the bar graph. Students will need to be able to see these estimates. Use the overhead transparency of the recording sheet to construct a bar graph (this should be done with the projector turned off so students only see the finished graph). Mark a square on the sheet for each estimate, depending on the number of places that are correct for that estimate. Continue until data from all the estimates has been represented on the bar graph.

For example, if the actual number is 275, and the estimates are

258   532   367   275   271   282   272   467   291

the bar graph will look like this figure:

9			
8			
7			
6	▒		
5	▒		
4	▒		
3	▒	▒	
2	▒	▒	
1	▒	▒	▒
	100s correct	100s and 10s correct	100s, 10s, 1s correct

Discussion

Discuss the bar graph: Why is it shaped the way it is? What estimates could it be? Can the actual number be determined from the graph?

Action

Allow students to revise their estimates. This is a good assessment of who understands place value and can read the bar graph. Graph new estimates. As the number of correct places increases, students should be able to determine the actual amount by comparing their estimates to the bar graph.

Repeat with a new container of things to estimate.

Extension

■ Have students make their own graph for one estimate. To do this they will need to know the actual amount of items in the container.

Place-Value Graphing

	100s Correct	100s and 10s Correct	100s, 10s, and 1s Correct
14			
13			
12			
11			
10			
9			
8			
7			
6			
5			
4			
3			
2			
1			

Guess My Number

Strands

- Numeration
- Logic

Materials

- None

Description of Lesson

Overhead projector   yes ☐   no ☑

Conceptual Level	Concrete ☐	Connecting ☐	Abstract ☑
Instructional Level	Exposure ☐	Practice ☑	Mastery ☐

Purpose

To practice place value and rounding skills. The lesson can serve as a quick assessment of those skills.

Note

This lesson can be used as a short filler once it has been learned. It can be played for as long or short a period as desired. Allow approximately fifteen minutes to learn and play the game initially.

Action

Think of a two-digit number (for example, 37) and tell the class, "My number rounded to the nearest ten is 40. Can you guess my number?"

Call on students to guess the number. In the example above if a student guessed 43, you would respond by saying, "You're right, 43 rounded to the nearest ten is 40, but that was not my number." If a student guessed 32, you would respond by saying, "32 rounded to the nearest ten would be 30, so my number couldn't be 32."

▼ Extension

- Repeat using three- and four-digit numbers. Write the clues on the chalkboard, for example, for 537 write, "Rounded to the nearest hundred my number is 500. Rounded to the nearest 10 my number is 540."

Number Search

Strands

- Numeration
- Logic
- Number Operations

Materials

- Overhead transparency of "Number Search" recording sheet (choose the one appropriate for your students)

Description of Lesson

Overhead projector　　yes ☑　　no ☐

Conceptual Level	Concrete ☐	Connecting ☐	Abstract ☑
Instructional Level	Exposure ☐	Practice ☑	Mastery ☐

Purpose

To explore the attributes of numbers within a problem-solving context.

Action

Ask students to write down a number less than 50 (or less than 1,000, depending on the recording sheet you use). On the overhead projector reveal one number clue at a time. Students give themselves a point if their number fits the clue. Discuss each clue as it is shared to be sure that everyone understands its meaning. After all clues have been shared, find out which student had the highest score.

Repeat the procedure using the same clues. With the overhead projector off, have the students select a new number. The students know what the clues are in advance but may not remember every one. Remind them to consider the clues in selecting their number.

Display all of the clues, and ask the students to try to come up with one number that will match all the clues (Number Search A is 35 and B is 72).

Discussion

Once the class has come to an agreement on what the number is, discuss which clues were the most helpful in determining the number. Could some clues have been eliminated? How many of the clues would be needed to find the number?

▼ Extensions

■ Have students create their own Number Searches. This is best done by starting with a number and then creating clues to match it. You may want to collect these and do one each day or have students exchange with one another.

■ You can easily create your own Number Searches to stress the skills and attributes of numbers appropriate for your students' needs. With middle school students, the Number Search might focus on prime numbers and divisibility rules, for example.

Number Search

Choose a number less than 50.

Give yourself a point for each clue your number matches.

A.   It is between 10 and 40.

B.   It is an odd number.

C.   It is greater than 20.

D.   It is a two-digit number.

E.   When you count by 5s you say this number.

F.   Both digits are odd.

G.   When you add the digits together, you get 8.

Name _____

Number Search

Choose a number less than 1,000.

Give yourself a point for each clue your number matches.

A.   It is between 50 and 600.

B.   It is more than a single-digit number.

C.   It is a multiple of 4.

D.   It is not a square number.

E.   It is an even number.

F.   It is evenly divisible by all single-digit numbers except 5 and 7.

G.   The sum of the digits is less than 10.

H.   It is less than 300.

I.   It contains an odd digit.

J.   All its digits are prime.

K.   The digits are in descending order.

L.   It is a factor of 144.

Place-Value Hockey

Strands

- Numeration
- Number Operations

Materials

- Masking tape
- Color Tiles

Description of Lesson

Overhead projector   yes ☐   no ☑

Conceptual Level	Concrete ☐	Connecting ☐	Abstract ☑
Instructional Level	Exposure ☐	Practice ☑	Mastery ☐

Purpose

To provide addition practice with large numbers and reinforce place-value understanding.

Preparation

On a tabletop lay out five strips of tape labeled 10s, 100s, 1,000s, 10,000s, and 100,000s at six-inch intervals. Put the strips in random order.

1,000s
100,000s
10s
100s
10,000s

Modeling

Demonstrate shooting a Color Tile by flicking it with your finger from the edge of the table and recording your score.

For example, if the tile passes the 10s tape strip but not the 100,000s tape, then the score for that tile would be 10.

Action

Have groups of students construct their own hockey-playing boards on their tables using masking tape. Have them take turns shooting, keeping track of their scores.

When everyone has taken ten turns, have them add up their scores. The player closest to one million is the winner.

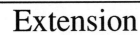

Extension

■ Play the game with scoring taking place after all ten tiles have been shot for each player. This allows players to bump the tiles of other players as in shuffleboard.

The Rounding Game

Strands

- Numeration
- Number Operations
- Logic

Materials

- Recording sheets
- Overhead transparency of recording sheet
- Regular dice (one for every two students)
- Rounding dice labeled 10, 100, 1000 (one for every two students)

Description of Lesson

Overhead projector   yes ☑   no ☐

Conceptual Level	Concrete ☐	Connecting ☐	Abstract ☑
Instructional Level	Exposure ☐	Practice ☑	Mastery ☐

Purpose

To provide practice adding and rounding numbers to the tens, hundreds, and thousands places.

Discussion

Review the places from ones to ten thousands. Give examples of numbers and ask students to round them to the tens, hundreds, thousands, or ten thousands place.

Modeling

Give each student a recording sheet, and place a recording sheet on the overhead projector. Establish a target number for the game, perhaps 100,000 or 200,000. The student closest to the target number at the end of the game will be the winner.

Roll a die and tell the class the result, for example, 5. Everyone places the digit 5 in one of the boxes in the first row under the "Actual Number" column. Numbers may not be moved once they have been placed.

Example:

Actual Number

	10,000s	1,000s	100s	10s	1s
Row 1:		5			

Continue to roll the die until each place, ten thousands through ones, has been filled in for the first row.

Example:

Actual Number

10,000s	1,000s	100s	10s	1s
3	5	2	6	2

Row 1:

Roll a rounding die, and tell the class the result, for example, 1,000. Students round the number in the first row to the nearest 1,000 and record the result in the first row under the "Rounded Number" column.

Actual Number						Rounded Number				
10,000s	1,000s	100s	10s	1s		10,000s	1,000s	100s	10s	1s
3	5	2	6	2	→	3	5	0	0	0

Action

Have students continue with partners until all seven rows are completed. Then have them add the numbers in the "Rounded Number" column to obtain their final score. The student whose total is closest to the target number is the winner.

Extensions

■ Discuss strategies for the placement of numbers.

■ Discuss the highest possible score and how it could be obtained.

The Rounding Game

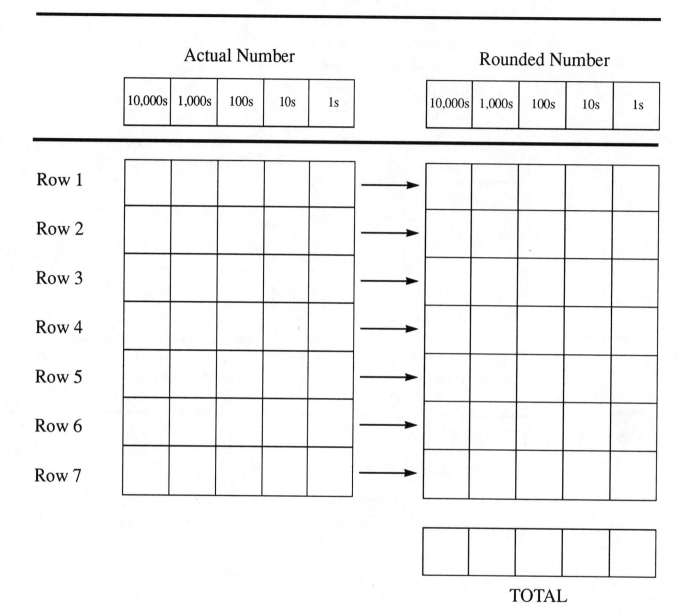

Actual Number

10,000s	1,000s	100s	10s	1s

Rounded Number

10,000s	1,000s	100s	10s	1s

Row 1

Row 2

Row 3

Row 4

Row 5

Row 6

Row 7

TOTAL

Make a Million

Strands

- Numeration
- Number Operations
- Estimation

Materials

- Recording sheet
- Newspapers
- Calculators (optional)

Description of Lesson

Overhead projector   yes ☐   no ☑

Conceptual Level	Concrete ☐	Connecting ☐	Abstract ☑
Instructional Level	Exposure ☐	Practice ☑	Mastery ☐

Purpose

To provide practice in addition and subtraction of large numbers while enhancing students' mental math and estimation skills.

Note

Although this activity is recommended for fourth through eighth graders, it can be used with second or third graders if number sense is stressed rather than computation. In this case, students should be given calculators to use.

Discussion

Tell students that today they will be exploring different combinations of numbers that add up to a million. Explain that they will be using their mental math abilities to help them do this.

Modeling

On the chalkboard (or overhead projector), model the procedure for the students. Tell them that the first example will be to come up with six numbers that add together to make one million. Tell the students that instead of using pencil and paper or calculators, they will be doing mental math.

Ask a student to give you a number, and write the number on the chalkboard. Call on a second student to give you another number to add to the one on the board. Write the number on the board and call on someone to give you an estimate of the total. Repeat this procedure until you have five addends on the board. Now ask students to discuss with their neighbors what number needs to be added to the group to make exactly a million. When all students have had time to discuss a response, call on a student to give you the final number. On the board, add the six addends together to verify the answer.

Activity

Select a number of addends to use, probably between four and ten. Divide the students up into teams with either four or five students to a team.

Have the first member of each team go to the chalkboard and write the first addend for his or her team on the board. Then have the next member go to the board and write a second addend and give an estimate for the sum of the numbers. Each successive member repeats this procedure by adding one more addend and giving an estimate. Depending on the number of addends, it may be necessary for some members of the team to go more than once. When it comes time to add the final addend, each team will discuss and agree on the number to be chosen for the final addend. When they have reached an agreement, one member of the team will go to the board, write the number, and perform the addition. Each team reaching exactly one million receives a point.

The "Make a Million" sheet can be used in the classroom or as homework. A bulletin-board display may be created with the numbers students cut out of the newspaper.

▼ ## Extensions

- Repeat the game with a different number of addends.

- The following constraints may be added to make the game more challenging:

  1. Assign the first addend for every group.

  2. Determine a range for every addend, for example, say that all addends must be between 1,000 and 200,000.

  3. Create a set of varying range cards and draw a different one for each round of play. A round would consist of one member from each team adding one addend to their team's tally.

  4. Make a set of cards marked 100,000, 200,000, 300,000, and so on, up to 900,000. After each round, draw a card and award a point to the team whose current total is closest to the number drawn.

  5. Make a set of cards marked 0 through 9. Before each round, draw a card. The student must then select an addend containing that digit.

Make a Million

1. Pick seven numbers that added together will total one million.

_____

_____

_____

2. How many thousands does it take to make a million? _____ Describe how you found this out.

_____

_____

_____

3. From newspapers or magazines, cut out ten numbers that you think will total 1,000,000. Paste them below and record them on the lines. Add them up.

Paste Numbers Here

_____

_____

_____

_____

_____

_____

_____

+ _____

Total

4. How far away were you from one million? _____

How Many Seconds Have You Lived?

Strands

- Numeration
- Estimation
- Number Operations
- Patterns

Materials

- Overhead transparency of recording sheet
- Recording sheet
- Calculators

Description of Lesson

Overhead projector   yes ☑   no ☐

Conceptual Level	Concrete ☐	Connecting ☐	Abstract ☑
Instructional Level	Exposure ☐	Practice ☑	Mastery ☐

Purpose

To provide students with a context in which to understand large numbers and their relative magnitudes. To use a calculator within a problem-solving context.

Discussion

Use the following questions to spark interest in the activity: How many seconds do you think you have lived? How would you find out how many seconds you have lived? What information would you need?

Modeling

Fill in the first year on the recording sheet, starting with the days column. Ask the class how many days are in a year. Ask the class how they can figure out the number of hours in a year. You may need to remind them that there are twenty-four hours in a day to get them thinking. Have them use calculators to figure out the number of hours in a year. Next, proceed as a class to fill in the minutes and seconds columns for the first year.

Move on to the ten-year row on the chart. Ask the class, "Do you know of any shortcuts to help us fill in the ten-year row on our chart?" If they do not recognize that every quantity in row one can be multiplied by ten, then allow them to work out each total and then look back for the patterns between rows one and ten.

The problem of leap years may come up. Have the class decide how to handle leap years. They may be ignored, each year may be counted as 365.25 days, one day may be added for every four years, and so on.

Action

Have students work independently to fill in the rest of the sheet using a calculator. Focus them on strategies for filling in the chart: "Using the information from years 1 and 10, what other years could you fill in? How? What will you do when the numbers will no longer fit on the calculator? When do you think that will happen?"

▼ Extensions

- Ask : How can you use this chart to help you figure out how many seconds you have lived? At what age will you have lived a billion seconds? (between 31 and 32 years). Will you ever live a trillion seconds? (No).

- *How Much Is a Million?*, by David Schwartz, explores the time it would take to count to a million, billion, and trillion. Students may compare this information with their chart of the seconds.

- *A Million Fish . . . More or Less,* by Patricia McKissack, is a tall tale in which many fantastic things happen to Hugh Thomas. Students may examine these events, such as jumping rope 5,553 times, to see just how long they would really take.

How Many Seconds Have You Lived?

Years	Days	Hours	Minutes	Seconds
1				
2				
3				
4				
5				
6				
7				
8				
9				
10				
11				
12				
13				
14				
15				

Where Are the Big Numbers?

Strands

- Numeration
- Estimation

Materials

- The front page of each newspaper section
- Recording sheet

Description of Lesson

Overhead projector yes ☑ no ☐

Conceptual Level	Concrete ☐	Connecting ☐	Abstract ☑
Instructional Level	Exposure ☑	Practice ☐	Mastery ☐

Purpose

To provide experience with large numbers in a real-world context that reinforces place-value understanding.

Discussion

Have the class name the sections of the newspaper. Ask them to speculate on which section would have the largest number in it, and ask them to give their reasons.

Action

Pass out recording sheets and have individuals fill in their predictions. Explain the place abbreviations to them, for example, "HB" stands for "hundred billions," "TB" for "ten billions," and so on. To each group or pair of students, pass out the front page of a section of the newspaper. Have them work together to locate the largest number they can find and fill in the appropriate line of the recording sheet. Have a student from each group go to the overhead projector and record the group's findings on the appropriate line of the overhead transparency. Have the groups record the information from other groups and complete the recording sheet.

Discussion

Have students discuss their results and share information about the numbers they located in their section.

▼ Extensions

- Repeat the exercise using a different newspaper.

- Start an ongoing bulletin board of large numbers.

- Use this activity as an opening in the morning. For a week, graph which newspaper sections have the largest numbers. See if large numbers appear more often in some sections than others.

- Read more about newspapers in *Hot Off the Press,* by Crismann, or *How Newspapers Are Made,* by Walters.

Name _____

Where Are the Big Numbers?

Which section of the newspaper do you think will have the biggest number in it?
Explain why you think so.

_____

_____

List the biggest number from the first page of each section of the paper.

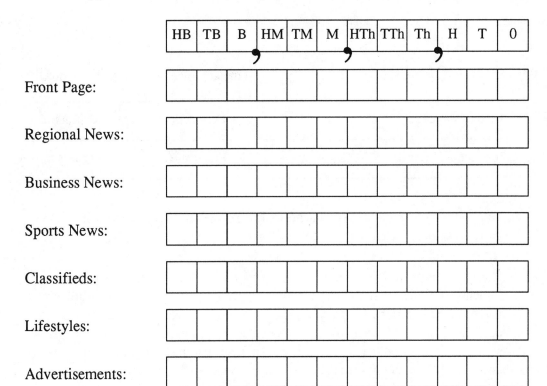

HB	TB	B	HM	TM	M	HTh	TTh	Th	H	T	0

Front Page:

Regional News:

Business News:

Sports News:

Classifieds:

Lifestyles:

Advertisements:

List the numbers above in order from least to greatest using the *less than* sign <.
For example: 3 < 5 < 12 < 49.

_____ < _____ < _____ <

_____ < _____ < _____ <

_____

You've Got the Answer

Strands

- Number Operations
- Numeration
- Estimation
- Logic

Materials

- A transparency of the sample "You've Got the Answer" recording sheet
- Recording sheets

Description of Lesson

Overhead projector   yes ☑   no ☐

Conceptual Level	Concrete ☐	Connecting ☐	Abstract ☑
Instructional Level	Exposure ☐	Practice ☑	Mastery ☐

Purpose

To provide an opportunity for students to develop operation sense and work backwards in a problem-solving context.

Discussion

Show the sample problem on the overhead projector. Read the situation to the students. Tell them that on this page the answer for all of the problems is already given but the questions are missing. Their job will be to come up with the questions that match the answers (for example, a question for "24" might be, "How many children are on the bus?"). Remind students that they should only use information from the situation and not add any additional information.

Using the sample problem, have the students come up with possible questions to match the answers.

Action

Give students a copy of the recording sheet. Allow them to work with partners to write questions that match the answers.

Discussion

Have students read some of their questions, and call on other members of the class to answer them.

▼ Extensions

- Create your own situations with answers, and have students write the questions.

- Allow students to make their own situations, and exchange them with each other.

You've Got the Answer
Sample Problem

A school bus holds 35 passengers and the driver. There are
16 girls on the bus and only half as many boys.

24

8

11

36

You've Got the Answer

In Mr. Maxwell's class, 17 students drink milk at lunch and 9 drink juice. Ms. Adams's class has 2 more students than Mr. Maxwell's class. Half of her students drink milk at lunch. Both Mr. Maxwell and Ms. Adams drink juice.

8

25

54

5

A Paper Million

Strands

- Numeration
- Estimation
- Number Operations

Materials

- The classified section of the newspaper cut into two-inch squares
- Calculators
- Recording sheets

Description of Lesson

Overhead projector   yes ☐   no ☑

Conceptual Level	Concrete ☐	Connecting ☐	Abstract ☑
Instructional Level	Exposure ☐	Practice ☑	Mastery ☐

Purpose

To provide experience with computational estimation and large quantities.

Modeling

On the chalkboard (or overhead projector) write a variety of numbers, ranging from three to five digits in length. Ask the class to estimate the sum of all the numbers. Discuss their estimation strategies and demonstrate the "lead-digit" method, which involves summing only the lead digits of each number. Discuss with the class that phone numbers, ZIP codes, and addresses are just strings of individual digits rather than complete numbers. (One good distinction is that numbers are used to quantify things, but series' of numbers are only used for identification.)

Action

Have each student select a two-inch square of newspaper. Have them complete their worksheets by referring to their squares.

Extension

- Have students create a bulletin board display of a "newspaper million" using the classified section.

A Paper Million

Look at your newspaper square. Which side of the square, the front or the back, do you think will contain the greater total when all the numbers are added together from that side? (Use that side to answer the rest of the questions.)

Circle, underline, or highlight all the numbers on the side you chose.

Estimate what you think the total of the numbers will be:

_____

Add all the numbers on this side of the square. Remember: phone numbers, ZIP codes, and addresses are considered strings of individual digits rather than complete numbers.

This would be a good time to use a calculator.

Actual Total:

_____

Glue your
newspaper square here.

A Paper Million

1. If you added the numbers on *both sides* of your square, what would you estimate the total to be?

   Explain your reasoning.

2. If you had five squares and added up the numbers on *one side* of each square, what would you estimate the total to be?

   Explain your reasoning.

3. If you had 10 squares? Explain.

4. If you had 100 squares? Explain.

5. How many squares do you think it would take to total at least one million?

   Explain your reasoning.

6. If you were to add up all the numbers on one whole page of the newspaper, what would you estimate the total to be?

   Explain your reasoning.

Who's Greatest?

Strands

- Numeration
- Estimation
- Number Operations
- Logic

Materials

- One die for every two players
- Recording sheets

Description of Lesson

Overhead projector   yes ☑   no ❏

Conceptual Level	Concrete ❏	Connecting ❏	Abstract ☑
Instructional Level	Exposure ❏	Practice ☑	Mastery ❏

Purpose

To provide practice with place value, addition, and ordering numbers within a problem-solving context.

Modeling

Demonstrate the game on the overhead projector.

Rules

The die is rolled and both players write the digit from the die in one of the place-value positions in row one. Players take turns rolling the die until all the place-value positions are filled in row one. The players determine which sign—less than, greater than, or equals—is correct for that row. The player with the larger number scores a point. Play continues until all lines are filled in on the page. Students find the sum of all their numbers, scoring a point for that row as usual. Then they total their points to determine the overall winner.

Action

Have students play the game. Watch for strategies as they play: this serves as a good assessment of their understanding of place value. Discuss strategies with the class after one game has been played.

Extensions

- Change the game so that the player having the least is the winner.

- Make it a subtraction game where the players each start with 500,000 and subtract to get to zero.

Who's Greatest?

Name _____

10,000s	1,000s	100s	10s	1s

< > =

Name _____

10,000s	1,000s	100s	10s	1s

Making Allowances

Strands

- Number Operations
- Numeration
- Algebra
- Patterns

Materials

- Recording sheet

Description of Lesson

		Overhead projector	yes ☐	no ☑

Conceptual Level	Concrete ☐	Connecting ☐	Abstract ☑
Instructional Level	Exposure ☐	Practice ☑	Mastery ☐

Purpose

To provide students with practice in addition and multiplication within a problem-solving investigation, and to expose them to a geometric growth sequence.

Discussion

Set up the investigation by telling a version of the following story:

Once upon a time there were twins, a boy and a girl. They fought all the time. One always claimed to be smarter than the other. Their parents were being driven crazy by all this arguing. One night the mother and father were discussing what to do about all the arguing and fighting. They had tried everything. Finally, the mother said she had an idea. "I will devise a test to figure out which one is smarter and settle this fighting once and for all."

But what kind of a test will it be?" asked the father.

"I will give each child a choice of allowances. The children will receive their allowances just once a year on their birthdays until they are 21. Their first option would be to receive $1,000 for every year old they are, each year until they are 21. Their other option would be to receive $1 on their first birthday, $2 on their second, $4 on their third, and so forth, doubling the amount each year until they are 21."

"Do we have that much money?" asked the father.

"It doesn't matter," said the mother, "It is only a test and the smarter child will know which option to choose."

"I better figure this out myself," said the father.

Ask students to make predictions about what they think will be the better choice.

Modeling

Model filling in the chart with the students. Make sure they know how to determine how much allowance each child is receiving. Ask them how to compute the total amount each child has received. Also model filling in the "Total Amount" column—the running total is useful in determining which option is better at any point.

Action

Students complete the chart to determine which is the better choice.

Extensions

- Read *The King's Chessboard* by David Birch to demonstrate the power of a geometric progression. Ask students how the story is like the allowance problem.

- Have students compare the two options by graphing them on a coordinate graph. The first option will produce a linear graph of the arithmetic progression. The second option will produce a parabolic graph of the geometric progression. Formulas may be derived as well.

  The progression for the second option is a logarithmic scale built on base two (see "The Richter Scale" for further explanation of logarithmic scales). This means that the year is the power to which 2 must be raised to obtain the allowance. For example, in year 6 the allowance would be 2^6, or $64, in year 8 the allowance would be 2^8, or $256.

- *If You Made a Million*, by David Schwartz, provides an opportunity to further explore aspects of money, such as interest.

Making Allowances

Year	Allowance (Option 1)	Total Amount	Allowance (Option 2)	Total Amount
1	$1,000	$1,000	$1	$1
2	$2,000	$3,000	$2	$2
3				
4				
5				
6				
7				
8				
9				
10				
11				
12				
13				
14				
15				
16				
17				
18				
19				
20				
21				

Assessing Learning

Authentic Assessment

Our goal has been to engage students in authentic mathematical tasks, games, and investigations that promote numeracy. How then do we best assess their progress in this development, evaluate our instruction, plan for the future, gather information for parents and guardians about their children's needs, and communicate to children about their progress?

Traditional forms of assessment, such as standardized tests, do not usually meet these objectives, nor do they focus on numeracy as we have come to understand it. Rather, they focus on students' computational skills, often in isolation. We must focus on alternative forms of assessment that will yield more useful information. To be useful, assessment must be aligned with the goals and objectives of the math curriculum and be ongoing. To be complete, assessment must draw on multiple sources of information. To be authentic, assessment must resemble real learning tasks and actively involve students.

What Do We Assess?

Focusing on numeracy, we must assess students' abilities to use and make sense of numerical information in a variety of contexts. Specifically, assessments should examine the students' abilities to construct relationships among and between numbers, make reasonable estimates of quantities and measurements, understand the effects of operations on numbers, collect and analyze data, understand and use place-value concepts, recognize mathematical patterns and relationships, communicate mathematical ideas, and illustrate mathematical concepts.

Ability to Construct Relationships Among and Between Numbers. A rich variety of connections between numbers provides students with the basis from which to work flexibly with numbers. It constitutes an individual's number sense. A demonstration of these relationships would include ordering and comparing numbers, counting with one-to-one correspondence, conservation of number, stating equalities ("give three other names for 12"), using known information to construct new information ("if you know that $5 \times 8 = 40$, how could you use this information to find 6×8?"), recognizing classes of numbers ("how are 3, 5, 7, and 2 alike?"), understanding class inclusion ("how many 20s are there is 67?"), and so forth.

Ability to Make Reasonable Estimates. Estimation skills draw on our internalized sense of numbers and experiences in quantifying the world around us. Estimation involves the use of known information in producing an estimate. In our assessment, we want to focus on the reasoning behind the estimate rather than only the accuracy. It is possible to guess correctly but not employ reasoning. Good reasoning in estimating may involve taking a sample, making comparisons to known information, visualizing, or drawing on prior knowledge.

Ability to Understand the Effects of Operations on Numbers. Understanding the effects of performing computational operations on numbers provides the basis for using computation to effectively solve problems and make sense of the solution.

It requires conceptual understanding rather than simply procedural knowledge. The question, "Which would make a number smaller: adding, subtracting, multiplying, or dividing by 2?" requires the student to make a generalization based on an understanding of the effect of these operations on numbers rather than perform any computation. The effects of operations on whole numbers and fractions may differ and require a full understanding of fractional numbers to make sense.

Ability to Collect and Analyze Data. Data collection and analysis involve using numbers to represent, inform, and help solve real problems and phenomena. Students need to be able to create their own graphs to display numerical information in the most effective format. This may involve the collection and organization of information either directly or indirectly. Students need to be able to formulate statistical questions, categorize and group information, represent data in a variety of contexts, interpret their findings, and draw conclusions.

Ability to Understand and Use Place-Value Concepts. A true understanding of place value provides students with the skill to devise their own computational algorithms and make sense of the traditional ones. Assessment should ask them to construct models of numbers and explain computational procedures.

Ability to Recognize Mathematical Patterns and Relationships. The ability to recognize patterns and relationships in mathematics empowers the learner to reconstruct, reinvent, and discover mathematics. Inductive reasoning is based on observable patterns. Patterns connect the entire body of mathematical knowledge.

Ability to Communicate Mathematical Ideas. A numerate individual is conversant in the language of mathematics and can communicate mathematical ideas to others. Students must be given opportunities to develop their ability to communicate mathematically just as their oral and written communication skills must be fostered. The communication of ideas is one of the best assessments of understanding. Communication is necessarily two-way and therefore involves an individual's ability to follow the reasoning and explanations of others.

Ability to Illustrate Mathematical Concepts. Conceptual knowledge cannot be assessed by observing the performance of procedures. Giving the solution to 4×3 does not necessarily indicate a full understanding of multiplication. To assess conceptual understanding, we must ask students to explain and illustrate these concepts.

How Do We Assess?

To be complete, assessment must utilize a variety of sources and methods of gathering information. Tests alone, no matter how well-constructed, cannot fully document a student's growth and understanding. Observation, interviews, performance assessments, students' self-reports, cooperative tests, individual tests, and portfolios of students' work are all valuable assessment tools. These assessment techniques must be interspersed throughout the year to provide a moving picture of a student's performance and progress rather than the single snapshot provided by tests.

These alternative forms of assessment are more time-consuming for both teachers and students. However, they do not detract from instruction as traditional tests often do but can actually be vehicles for additional instruction and growth. This merging of instruction and assessment is one benefit of alternative assessment strategies. Students must be made aware of both how and what you will be assessing. The information you collect from observations, interviews, and portfolios must be shared with students in order for them to become actively engaged in their own learning. Information gained from alternative forms of assessment can be valuable to students in shaping their behavior and monitoring their progress. When students know that they will be evaluated on how well they can work within a group, they are more likely to develop the skills you have indicated to be important.

Observation. As teachers, we daily utilize our observation skills to monitor students' understanding and adjust our instruction accordingly. However, in using observation as an assessment tool, we must focus our observation more sharply on individual students and their behavior. Such focused observations cannot go on in the midst of instruction but would need to occur as students work independently or in small groups. Instruction that consists primarily of independent drill and practice on worksheets would not offer a very rich environment for observation. In contrast, all the lessons in this book and the mathematical investigations that you might design will provide ample opportunities for probing observation.

To better focus your observation, it is best to try to observe only three to five students in any one lesson and to limit the scope of your observations. You might focus on the student's problem solving, reasoning, communication of mathematical ideas, estimation skills, or flexibility in dealing with numbers as appropriate for the lesson in which the observation is taking place. A checklist can often be helpful in structuring observations and keeping records. It must not be too broad and should include space for short comments about the student's performance. In any one lesson, you are not likely to see all of the categories on your list in each student's performance. The following checklists can be used in a variety of settings and grade levels.

Date _____

Observational Assessment Checklist
Communication and Cooperation

S = Strong   Task Observed _____
D = Developing
W = Weak
N = Not Observed

Communication	Name of student	Name of student	Name of student
Listens to and follows others' reasoning.			
Incorporates others ideas in planning a solution strategy.			
Explains own ideas and supports position with evidence.			
Asks questions of others to facilitate own understanding.			

Cooperation			
Shares responsibility; supports and encourages others.			
Assumes personal responsibility within the group. Becomes actively involved.			

Date _____

Observational Assessment Checklist
Problem Solving

S = Strong   Task Observed_____
D = Developing
W = Weak
N = Not Observed

Understanding	Name of student	Name of student	Name of student
Understands the task at hand and/or clarifies understanding with others before beginning.			

Problem-Solving Skills

Devises a plan before beginning work on a solution.			
Organizes information to facilitate problem solving.			
Recognizes and self-corrects flaws in planning, reasoning, and computation. Shows the ability to adapt and work flexibly.			
Judges reasonable- ness of solution.			

Persistence

Persists in investigation even when encountering difficulties.			

138

While it is important to have a planned focus for your observation, you must also allow yourself the flexibility to note and attend to other significant behaviors from both the students you are observing and other individuals. The traits you select to focus on in making your observations should be characteristics that cannot be assessed as well using other techniques. The processes involved in doing math, solving problems, communicating, and working within a group are particularly appropriate for observational assessments as these are difficult if not impossible to assess any other way. Information about the specific knowledge a student possesses would be better assessed through interviews or tests.

Interviews. Interviews are extremely valuable tools for gathering information about students' understanding of mathematical ideas. In one-on-one conferences, you are able to probe students' understanding, which goes well beyond correct answers on tests. While interviews are one of the best sources of information, they are time consuming. The question of what to do with the rest of class is a major concern in conducting one-on-one interviews. To free yourself up, have the rest of the class do independent work conducting their own investigations, free exploring new manipulatives, working at predetermined math stations, playing math games, or working at the computer. Schools and administrators wishing to support alternative assessment might use administrators, support staff, and classroom aids to free up classroom teachers to conduct interviews.

Because of the time constraints involved, conferences must be well-planned and focused. If the entire class is to be interviewed, it will be important to deal with a narrowly defined topic, such as conservation of number, that can be dealt with in under five minutes. In-depth interviews might only take place with a few individuals from whom you need more information to better plan instruction. It is important to record your findings during the interview in a clear and concise manner. Short anecdotal records work well. A video camera or cassette recorder may also be used.

The interview technique can also be employed while students are working independently. While observing the students at work, question a student to further probe his or her thinking. The questioning should only temporarily interrupt the student's work at hand. Such on-the-spot assessment can be quite valuable in checking students' understanding of the task at hand.

Within the structured interview, you can ask students to illustrate or represent concepts, explain operations or procedures, make generalizations, or extend their thinking. Some examples follow:

Illustrations and Representations of Concepts

- Draw a picture to show what 3×4 means.

- Use Base Ten Blocks to show 4,529.

- Use marbles to show 1/3 of a group.

- With these red and yellow tiles, show the ways you can represent the number 6.

- Using Base Ten Blocks, show what 1.3×0.4 means.

A particularly effective assessment of place-value understanding that asks students to make a representation of the concept was designed by Kamii and Lewis (1990). Students are shown a card on which the numeral 16 is written and asked to read the numeral and count out 16 chips. The interviewer then draws an imaginary circle around the 6 in the numeral 16 and asks the child to use the chips to show what this part means. Next the interviewer draws an imaginary circle around the 1 in the numeral 16 and asks the child to show with the chips what this part means. The term "this part" is used to avoid using words that might signify the correct response. If the child does not show ten chips to represent the 1 ten, then the interviewer questions the child further to account for the remaining chips that were part of the original set of 16. "You used all these chips to show 16, you used these chips to show this part (circles the 6) and this one to show this part (circles the 1). What about the rest of these chips? Is this the way it's supposed to be or is something strange going on here?"

Kamii (1990) found that only 15 percent of students taught in a traditional manner with textbooks, worksheets, and manipulatives were successful in representing place-value concepts in this interview. And yet, this same group of students had an average score of 97.6 percent on an achievement test of place value. Clearly, the test was not an adequate indicator of students' understanding of place value. The interview provided invaluable information on students' weaknesses and misconceptions about our place-value system.

Explanations of Operations and Procedures

- Read 8 – 3. What other ways could you read it?

- Add 27 + 38 and explain each step as you perform it.

- Describe a situation in which you would need to use division.

- Explain what happens when you find an average.

Asking students to give explanations of operations and procedures can often be done as students are working independently; a formal interview is not needed. Asking students to explain their reasoning is a good instructional technique because it lets them know that you value understanding and expect them to be able to make sense out of the procedures they perform.

Generalizations

- Do you have a rule for subtracting 0? Why does your rule work?

- Do you have a rule for multiplying by 1? Why does your rule work?

- How do addition and subtraction go together?

- How is multiplication like addition?

- Does 3 + 5 + 8 = 5 + 3 + 8? Why? Do you think this would work with other numbers? Why?

Conservation of number tasks involve a special type of generalization in which students must recognize that no matter how a group of objects is arranged, the quantity does not change. Students must generalize this understanding from previous experiences with quantities. While conservation of number is a task that Piaget found most children acquired between the ages of five and seven, children who have difficulty making sense of place-value concepts and seem generally

Making Numbers Make Sense

confused by work with numbers may not yet possess conservation of number. Programs that require students to begin abstract work with numbers too soon do not provide students with the experiences they need to generalize the concept of conservation. While maturity plays a large part, appropriate experiences and interaction with peers to discuss these developing concepts are important.

Conservation occurs first with small quantities and gradually increases until the child is able to generalize to all numbers. Therefore, assessments should begin with small quantities (between six and ten objects) and progress to larger quantities (between twenty-five and forty objects). It is not necessary to assess higher quantities, as children will have made the generalization to all numbers.

To assess conservation of number, ask the student to count out a specific number of objects, then rearrange the objects and ask the student if there are more, less, or the same amount. Students who do not yet possess conservation of number will be influenced by their perception and will state that there are more if the objects have been spread out and less if they have been pushed together. It is not possible to teach conservation. As a teacher you want to provide opportunities to count, order, and group objects in a meaningful way. Those who try to teach by telling the student will be able to produce correct responses but will not be able to communicate understanding.

Extensions of Thinking: Building on the Known

- If you know that $5 \times 8 = 40$, how could you find 6×8 ?

- How many two-number combinations are there that make 4? How would you figure out how many combinations there are to make 10?

- If this room is 30 feet long, how wide would you estimate the room to be?

Kathy Richardson (1990) has designed an assessment of students' number relationships that involves building on information about a known quantity. Specifically, it assesses the student's ability to use counting on as a strategy. Counting on involves an understanding of class inclusion, that the quantity 6 is included within the quantity 8. Students build an understanding of number inclusion through meaningful counting and grouping experiences. They come to realize that 1 is part of 2, 2 part of 3, 3 part of 4, and so on.

In Richardson's assessment, appropriate for grades one through three, students are presented with four Unifix® Cube trains of various lengths from eight to fourteen and in differing colors. Students are asked to count one row of cubes and then asked about the other Unifix® trains, "If the brown train is nine long, how long is the yellow train? The green train? The red train?" Students who have a sense of number inclusion will employ counting on from the known quantity of nine to figure out the length of the other trains. Students who do not possess this sense of number inclusion will simply count each of the trains beginning with one. While the counting on strategy can be taught, students will not use it until it makes sense to them and they have developed number inclusion.

Performance. It is important that assessments resemble authentic mathematical tasks. If instruction is focused on understanding and developing numeracy, then assessment must reflect this. To use only traditional tests that focus on the memorization of procedures would be counterproductive. Students will work for what is rewarded, so our assessments must reward understanding.

Performance assessments ask students to engage in mathematical problem solving or investigations either individually, with a partner, or in a small group. The investigations may be limited to a single class period or may represent an extended project that students pursue over time. In a performance assessment, the students may be observed and questioned while they work. In addition, the students are asked to produce either a written explanation of how they solved the problem or completed the investigation, or to produce some type of finished project such as a plan, report, or graph.

One performance assessment designed for sixth graders focused on creating a *Consumer Reports*-type article. The students had been engaged in a three-week study of unit pricing. This study provided a context in which students could practice their long-division skills. The focus throughout the unit was on using information to make wise consumer decisions.

As the unit progressed, it became apparent that informed decisions are based on more than just unit price: taste, nutritional value, and various personal considerations all play a role. *Zillions: The Consumer Reports Magazine for Kids* provided examples of how a variety of information is needed to make an informed decision about a product. Having groups of students conduct a taste test and write a magazine article provided an authentic way to assess their abilities to apply their skills in context and make informed decisions based on the information available. A blackline master outlining the assignment follows.

Note: Care must be taken to consider food allergies or dietary restrictions when using food in the classroom.

What's Best?

Informed Consumers Report

Your group will work together to create an article for our own class version of *Consumer Reports* that incorporates what you have learned during our study of unit pricing. You will choose a food or beverage category to review and evaluate for your article. You will need to select a category that has several different varieties. For example, "carrots" is not a category, but "vegetables" is.

In order to rate the items in your food or beverage category, you will design a taste test of the items. To do this, you will need to prepare samples of each item for each member of the class to taste. You will need to design some type of form on which the tasters will rate each item according to a scale you determine. You will carry out the taste test in class.

You may want to review articles in *Zillions* and *Consumer Reports* to help you in writing your article. Your article must contain:

1. Background information such as the product's or food's history, its popularity, or how it is produced.

2. A description of how the products were evaluated and by whom.

3. A summary of the results of the tests.

4. An eye-catching chart or table of the results of the taste test as well as information on the price per unit and per serving. You may want to include additional information regarding calories and nutrition. Within your group you will need to assign specific jobs to each individual. While the group must work together and share ideas and information to be successful, someone should be in charge of (1) collecting and organizing data, (2) carrying out the taste test, and (3) researching and writing the article.

Your group's finished article will be graded based on its level of interest to the reader, organization, thoroughness, spelling, punctuation, and presentation of data in the chart or table.

Students' Self-Reports. Asking students to evaluate and write about their progress in mathematics can provide additional information about affective issues related to the learning of mathematics. In addition, it helps to involve students in monitoring their own progress and causes them to take an active role. Too many students have the view that learning is something that is done to them rather than something they control. By actively involving students in monitoring their progress you can enable them to take more initiative and personal responsibility.

Journals are an effective format for older students to reflect upon their learning. Journals may be used daily for note-taking and reflection. Writing about mathematics is a good way for individuals to consolidate their understanding. Students may be asked to write a summary of what they have learned following a unit of study. Such writing, whether done as part of an ongoing journal or as a specific assignment, provides assessment information and helps students develop skills in communicating mathematically.

A personal mathematics autobiography written by students at the beginning of the year provides insights into what students think mathematics is. It provides information about their attitudes and feelings as well. A second autobiography written at the end of the year serves as a nice assessment of your ability as a teacher to encourage positive attitudes and change perceptions about mathematics.

Cooperative and Individual Tests. If students are routinely encouraged to work cooperatively as members of a group or learning team, they must also be given the opportunity to take tests as a team as well as individually. To give tests only to individuals sends a mixed message that what really counts is individual performance. Students will consequently be reluctant to work cooperatively and effectively with others when such work is not valued enough to be assessed.

In both cooperative and individual tests, students should be asked to demonstrate understanding and not just recall of procedures. While it is necessary to test both procedural knowledge and conceptual knowledge, assessment of students' understanding of concepts should be the first priority. After it has been established that students understand concepts, then it is appropriate to direct attention to developing and later assessing procedural skills. An overall assessment plan will make sure that assessment is balanced to include both procedural and conceptual understanding.

Open-ended questions that require students to write their own solutions and explanations should be used, as well as high-quality multiple-choice questions that require more time and thought to answer. Some examples of open-ended questions that test conceptual understanding follow:

This problem can be done in a variety of ways but primarily assesses students' understanding of place value.

1. Place the digits 1, 2, 3, 4, and 5 in the boxes below to create a multiplication problem with the largest possible product.

$$\begin{array}{c}\boxed{}\ \boxed{}\ \boxed{}\\ \times\ \boxed{}\ \boxed{}\end{array}$$

This assesses students' abilities to recognize mathematical patterns and relationships.

2. What will the 10th building in this series look like? Describe it.

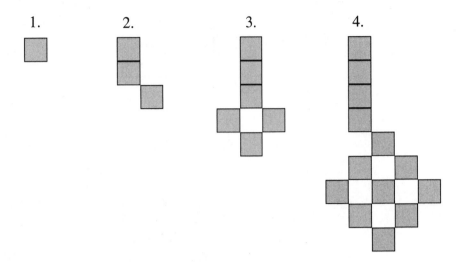

1.   2.   3.   4.

Asking students to create their own test questions forces them to make judgments and evaluations about the concepts they have learned.

3. Make up three questions to determine whether a student understands decimals. Make up one easy, one medium, and one hard question. Explain why you labeled the question as easy, medium, or hard.

This question asks students to apply their understanding of order of operations in a real-world context.

4. Write an equation that matches the story below. The equation should contain only the original numbers (that means don't do any of the work in your head). Once you have written the equation, solve it step-by-step using the order of operations rule.

> In the hospital, Sam was given 3 pills in the morning and 2 in the afternoon and 1 at bedtime. This went on for 4 days. On the fifth day he was dismissed after taking his afternoon pills. Altogether, he took 29 pills.

Rather than solve the equation, students are asked to make sense of it mathematically by putting it in context.

5. Write a story to match the equation below:

$$7 \times (4 + 5) - 6 = 57$$

This question asks students to interpret graphical information.

6. Kara conducted a survey of her classmates and made the following graph. What question do you think she asked her classmates? How might this information be used?

								Board Games
								Computer Games
								Play Sports
								Watch TV
								Read
								Play Outside

Portfolios of Students' Work. Portfolios are increasingly being used as a comprehensive assessment tool in many locations for both language arts and mathematics. Portfolios need not be confined to any one discipline, but can be used as a tool to document learning across all disciplines. Portfolios serve as repositories of students' work. They are ongoing and may become part of a student's permanent file that is passed on from grade to grade. When information is gathered consistently over time, an organized, descriptive picture of the learning that has taken place emerges.

Both students and teachers should be involved in selecting the work that goes into a portfolio collection. The work may represent the best of a student's mathematical products as well as representative samples of work to show progress. In selecting what goes into a portfolio we should ask: What does this mathematical activity, product, or investigation tell me about the student as a mathematician? Will this information add to what is already known? How does this information reflect change and/or progress in the student's mathematical thinking and understanding?

Portfolios need not be standardized to serve as good assessment tools. There should be adequate leeway for students and teachers to select meaningful work. Producing work specifically for inclusion in the portfolio is not necessary. Rather, the curriculum should be rich enough to provide ample products for the portfolio. Such products must represent authentic mathematical tasks.

The blackline master on the following page asks students to begin work on producing a portfolio, assuming they have saved all their previous work, products, investigations, homework, quizzes, and tests in folders kept in the classroom.

Creating Your Portfolio

Throughout the year we will stop and look back on the work you have done. You will select samples of work that you feel represent your progress in the learning of mathematics to go into your portfolio. At the end of the year we will have put together a collection of samples that are representative of you as a mathematician.

To begin, look back over your work from this term. This should include homework, classwork, and tests. Select four to five items that you feel do a good job of reflecting your progress and work in math this term. These may be hard problems that you felt good about solving, a homework assignment, a challenge problem that interested you, or a problem you enjoyed solving. These do not have to be whole assignments. You might choose a particular problem from a test, homework, or class. If it was something from class that we did, you could write up an explanation of what it was and include that.

On each item you select, attach a note telling why you chose to include that piece of work to represent you.

Next, after you have selected your items to include in your portfolio, write a one-page summary of your work this term. Here are some things you might include in your summary:

What you learned.

What you had trouble understanding, which you want to work on in the future.

What you enjoyed.

What was important to you.

What you think will be important to you in the future.

How you're feeling about your progress.

What topics or ideas you are interested in exploring.

Finally, when you're done, have a parent or guardian review your portfolio. Ask him or her to write a paragraph responding to your work, progress, and learning so far this year.

Portfolios serve as an excellent vehicle for communicating with parents and can serve as the foundation for student-teacher conferences, student-parent conferences, and parent-teacher conferences. A one-on-one conference to review the portfolio with the student should allow both the teacher and the student to gain insight into how the student operates as a mathematician. In addition, the conference should serve as a vehicle both to support the student's progress and identify specific goals to be worked on in the future. The portfolio conference allows the student to take more responsibility and initiative for his or her learning. For parents, the portfolio conference provides much more detailed information about their child's progress and understanding of mathematics than grades alone.

Incorporating all these assessment techniques takes time and commitment. There is no special training needed to employ them, just ongoing practice and reflection. It would be helpful to begin your foray into alternative assessment with a colleague or group of colleagues with whom you can discuss and share your findings. Whatever you attempt, you will dramatically increase the amount of useful information you have about students.

Reporting to Parents

Assessment is used in a variety of ways: to inform instruction, to diagnose students' difficulties, to document performance and understanding, to evaluate the program and curriculum, and to assign grades. Alternative assessment strategies have a place in meeting all these goals. However, the issue of grading is perhaps one of the more complex goals and deserves special attention.

The purpose and usefulness of grades is increasingly being challenged, particularly at the elementary level. Grades provide us with little information on what a student knows and understands. While grades may motivate good students to perform and study for tests, they do not promote real learning as an end itself. Furthermore, students who receive poor grades often become even less motivated to pursue learning.

Throughout the country individual schools, districts, and states are devising alternative reporting systems that provide parents and students with better information about students' progress and understanding in a less evaluative manner. Narrative comments along with checklists of specific attributes and skills are taking the place of a single letter grade to describe students' performance. Below is one such comment form for third grade students. In each category, students are rated as either **S** for "Strong," **D** for "Developing," **W** for "Weak," or **N** for "Not Observed."

MATHEMATICAL SKILLS

Identifies mathematical patterns and relationships	
Demonstrates an understanding of numeration place value	
Constructs and interprets graphs	
Applies estimation skills	
Applies new concepts in solving problems	
Uses stategies to make reasonable responses	
Works flexibly with mathematical materials	
Demonstrates computational skills	

Such a change in reporting requires considerable parent education. Educating them about what mathematics is, how their children acquire mathematical understanding, and how they can be supportive should be one of our missions as educators. To continue to give letter grades because they are familiar forms of evaluation is shortsighted. Still, many teachers will be forced to give grades for years to come. If you must give grades, it is important that you communicate to students exactly how their grades will be determined. Make sure your grading process reflects your values in teaching for understanding. A balanced grading system would incorporate students' participation, homework assignments, projects, group work, and individual work. It should emphasize students' conceptual understanding over procedural knowledge.

Using Standardized Tests

While the focus of this chapter is on developing assessment techniques more aligned with our goal of fostering numeracy, it is acknowledged that the traditional standardized test is likely to be with us for quite some time. Many educators would like to see such tests banished, but our energies are perhaps better focused on making sure these tests are used more judiciously. If we recognize that standardized tests provide just one piece of information about a student or educational program and not the total picture, we can use them as a portion of an overall assessment program.

The testing industry is devoting substantial resources to the revision of the standardized tests that they market. Many test manufacturers are making plans to incorporate the wider view of mathematics called for in the NCTM *Standards*. Currently, between sixty and seventy percent of the questions on standardized tests deal with number operations (California Mathematics Council 1986). The revised tests are an attempt to assess understanding as well as computational skills through the use of more open-ended questions. The term "high-quality multiple-choice" is often being used to describe these types of questions. They differ from the traditional multiple-choice question in that they require more thought and time on the part of the student. Traditionally, multiple-choice questions on standardized tests are designed to take less than sixty seconds to read and answer. Given such time constraints, only factual knowledge and recall can be tested, not a student's ability to think and understand.

While the tests may begin to undergo changes, we must recognize that they will still possess significant shortcomings as true measures of a student's understanding and abilities. Because of their limited scope, they will still only measure a small portion of the curriculum, even though this may become more balanced and in line with our priorities.

The biggest drawback we must be aware of is that most standardized tests are norm-referenced, so each student's performance is measured against that of a reference group. In most cases this is a group of initial test-takers at the same grade level. This norming group serves as the standard to which future students are compared. In producing the norms, a normal distribution, or bell curve, of scores is created. Such a distribution places 50 percent of the students above average and 50 percent below, regardless of their true understanding.

Administrators, school boards, and legislatures demand that test scores increase in a testing system that mandates that half of all students be labeled "below average." Numerate citizens should challenge these demands. We must also question the assumption that a student who scores at the 24th percentile (meaning that he or she is above 24 percent of the test takers) has not been learning a substantial amount of mathematics during the year. In order to produce a normal distribution of scores, time is usually introduced as a factor to ensure that some students who know the material will not be able to finish the test and will therefore score more poorly than they would have otherwise.

Norm-referenced tests that seek to compare individuals can be misleading and distort the learning process. By comparing individuals one against the other, they do not account for individual differences in the pace of learning. This is particularly important during elementary school when developmental differences are at their greatest. Learning is not a race. Learning your multiplication table in third grade will not make you a better mathematician than someone who learns them in fourth grade. Such comparisons of individuals artificially produce winners and losers when what should exist is a community of learners. We should seek to develop passion for learning if we want our students to be competitive.

In most cases, it is individual teachers who place the pressure on themselves in regard to standardized testing. In an effort to prepare students for the test, some teachers rush through the curriculum at a pace that can only allow for superficial understanding. Students may be able to hold on to this information just long enough to do satisfactorily on the test, but the gains are short-lived and soon evaporate. Alternative forms of assessment won't make these students appear any better, but will show how shallow their understanding actually is. In contrast, the students of teachers who teach for understanding do just as well or better on standardized tests than students who have been taught for the test. It is not a question of either doing well on the tests or teaching for understanding.

Standardized tests do not provide much useful information about our students' mathematical literacy, and often mask many misunderstandings, but even so, students who have been taught to focus on understanding mathematics will generally do well on such tests. It is when these tests come to drive the curriculum that they can be harmful to students' learning. Teachers must not wait for the tests to change to begin making changes in their instruction. Alternative forms of assessment will provide teachers, parents, and students the information needed to support changes in both the curriculum and instruction.

The power of alternative forms of assessment is that they drive the curriculum and instruction to higher levels and thus students' achievement to higher levels. Alternative forms of assessment will most benefit the truly creative individual whose talent is not captured by standardized tests. For the majority of students, alternative forms of assessment will require more, not less, hard work and understanding. Authentic learning is at the same time more satisfying, complex, and challenging than rote mimicry of others' ideas and information.

Projects:

Highlighting Numeracy

An All-School Emphasis

In most schools, students begin the year studying and reviewing numeration topics such as place value and estimating. These topics allow teachers to assess the numeracy skills of their students and plan appropriate lessons to meet their needs. This also provides the context for a schoolwide emphasis on numeracy.

Rather than a mathematics fair at the end of the year centering around geometry or measurement, a project at the beginning of the year in exploring numeracy has the advantage of matching the current curriculum and setting the tone for mathematics work throughout the year. You can use the lessons in this book to promote investigations throughout the school. There are appropriate lessons for kindergarten through eighth grade.

An all-school assembly could be planned to allow classes to share their findings. Classes may make posters that reflect the findings of their various investigations. A few students from each class might report on the type of work they did and what they found out. Outside speakers, perhaps parents, might relate how they use mathematics in their daily work.

An assembly will motivate both you and your students. Families may be invited as a way to promote mathematics both at home and at school.

As a means of promoting social interaction in the learning of mathematics, classes can be paired with other grade levels. The combination of fourth grade with kindergarten, fifth with first, and sixth with second works well. The four-year difference assures that older students are mature enough to be of help to the younger students. Older students can help their "buddies" with many of the lessons in this book and then use the data they have gathered to extend the investigation in their classrooms. The whole school may create their own version of David Schwartz's book *How Much Is a Million?*

Collecting a Million

Models of large numbers are an extremely useful tool for developing understanding and creating mental images of numbers. Collecting a million of something gives students a firsthand experience of watching numbers increase. It also gives them an opportunity to engage in ongoing counting activities, estimating, record keeping, and graphing within a natural context.

The tabs from soft drink cans are an inexpensive and easy for students to collect. The cans themselves can be collected and recycled as part of a community service project and in conjunction with related activities in science.

Pennies might also be collected. While a million pennies is ten thousand dollars, on a day-to-day basis parents are usually willing to part with the spare pennies they have accumulated. According to a report in *Newsweek* magazine (January 7, 1991), the average family has nearly one thousand unused pennies in its possession. As an alternative, the goal might be to collect only one hundred thousand or just ten thousand pennies rather than a million.

Pennies also provide an opportunity to explore money and coin conversions. Many of the lessons in this book use pennies as a means of exploring numeracy. In the classroom, they serve as an inexpensive manipulative with a multitude of uses. Pennies may be counted, estimated, graphed, weighed, measured, grouped, exchanged, and so on.

The second graders in Mitzi Pearlman's and Lola Todd's classes (at Acres Green Elementary School in Littleton, Colorado, and Summit Elementary School in Highlands Ranch, Colorado) created a book of one million holes by using the "crusts" from the edges of tractor-fed computer paper. These bands were cut into strips containing ten holes, making them easier for young students to count. Five hundred holes were glued and laminated on each page. The finished book, titled *A Hole Million*, contains two thousand pages, weighs ninety-five pounds, and is two feet tall.

Regardless of what is collected, it will be a long-term project, perhaps two or more years. Every classroom should have its own container for the collection. Watching their individual contributions add up on a daily basis is motivating for young students. Also, by having the container in the classroom, the items are a readily available manipulative for mathematical investigations. To avoid re-counting and to help keep a constant tally of the items (pennies for example), use a small jar to collect the new pennies that students bring to class. When the jar has nine pennies in it, have the student putting in the tenth one dump the pennies into the large container and color in a square on a piece of ten-by-ten grid paper. The chart on the following page can be used to count by tens, with each row and column representing one hundred and the entire chart a thousand pennies. The chart is a good way to reinforce place-value concepts and provide experience in grouping by ten.

1,000 Pennies Chart

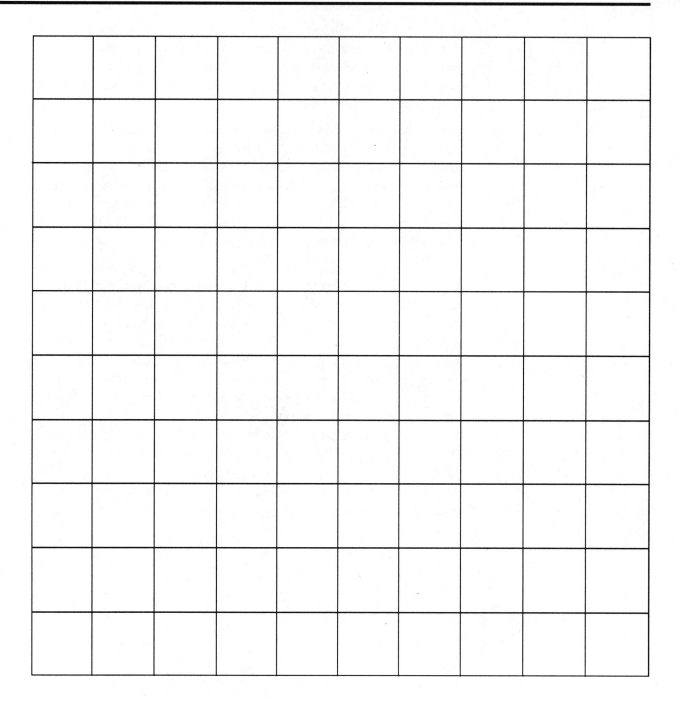

10

100

While collecting a million exists as a goal, the pennies or soft drink tabs can be used in numerous ways to reinforce numeracy. A sampling of activities are listed below for use with pennies, though many could be adapted for use with tabs or any other item being collected.

Estimating:

1. Estimate the number of pennies it will take to fill the container (a 1-gallon container will hold approximately 5,000 pennies).

2. Estimate the length of time it will take to fill the container or to collect a million pennies.

3. Estimate the number of pennies you can grab in one handful.

Graphing:

1. Graph pennies according to their mint date.

2. Graph the number of pennies brought in by different classes.

Measurement:

1. Estimate the length of the pennies laid end-to-end, and then measure them.

2. Estimate and figure out the height if the pennies were stacked.

3. How much would your weight in pennies be worth?

Social Studies:

1. Pull out a penny and tell (or research) something that happened the year it was minted.

2. Find out what year pennies were first minted.

3. Find out where pennies are minted.

4. Find out what other countries have pennies and compare them to the value of the United States penny.

5. Find out where copper and zinc for pennies is mined.

6. Debate whether or not the government should continue to mint pennies.

7. Find out when the mint switched from copper to zinc in pennies.

Art:

1. Find out what pictures have been on pennies.

2. Design a new penny.

Bulletin Boards

To keep track of schoolwide progress in collecting a million, a bulletin board display can be made similar to the charts in individual classrooms. On the school-wide chart, each small square represents one thousand. Thus, when students fill in a chart in the classroom, they can mark a square for their class on the schoolwide chart. Decorate the bulletin board with posters displaying various investigations individual classes or students have engaged in with pennies.

A glass window might also serve as a display. The window can be painted as a large collection jar. Large paper pennies, each representing a thousand pennies, added to the jar by taping them to the window.

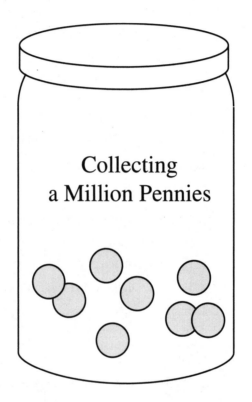

Collecting
a Million Pennies

Taking a Census

Conducting an all-school census provides students with the opportunity to collect and analyze data on questions of interest to them. Individual classes may contribute questions to the census or it may be patterned after the United States census. Information on the United States census can be obtained by contacting the Department of Commerce, Bureau of the Census, 14th and Constitution Ave. NW, Washington, DC 20230 or your state's local branch.

Setting up a schoolwide census requires advance planning. Students should first learn about the history of the census, which dates to Roman times. A census is literally a "count." What is counted depends on the needs and interests of the community administering the census. Native Americans took a census to gain information about their communities and plan for the upcoming winter. In the Phillips Petroleum-sponsored video *Challenge of the Unknown* there is a sequence on the 1982 census in China (Crimmins 1986).

As members of their school community, students should be encouraged to think of questions that might help the school to plan and make decisions for the future. Questions about after-school services are one example of this type of information. Students might ask questions related to their studies during the year. For example, if students study Mexico, they may want to ask how many classmates have been to Mexico or how many people speak Spanish. In addition, students would enjoy finding out silly or unusual information such as how many of them have fathers who are bald.

Once students have selected questions for the census, these questions can be put together into a census form. A day should be established for sending the census home and a date set for its return. The United States census seeks over a 99 percent return rate on census forms. This will be hard to replicate in the school setting. Once the data is returned, each class can construct a graphical analysis of the information to share on a schoolwide bulletin board.

A sample census is on the following page. Your own students will be more invested if they have a say in producing their own questions, however.

Taking a Census

1. How many people live in your household?	6. How many people in your family wear glasses or contact lenses?
2. How many children in your family? You may include those who no longer live at home.	7. How many pairs of brown, blue, green, and hazel eyes are in your family? Brown Blue Green Hazel
3. How many female members are in your household?	8. How many people who live at your house have ever been to Mexico?
4. How many male members are in your household?	9. What countries did your ancestors come from?
5. How many pets are in your household?	10. List the first letter of each family member's name.

Communicating to Parents

Schools cannot build numeracy alone, any more than they can build literacy alone. Parents and guardians must be made aware of the curriculum that their children will be exposed to in mathematics and how they can reinforce these experiences at home. Schools have a responsibility to keep parents informed, whether or not parents participate actively in their children's education.

A monthly mathematics newsletter to parents may be used for this purpose. Each newsletter might feature a description of a few of the activities classes have been engaged in during the past month. Students can write these for the newsletter. A column describing how children learn mathematics or detailing a particular mathematical strand, such as estimation, may be written by a teacher or principal. The NCTM *Standards* would provide an excellent resource for such a column. A regular feature written by parents or other outside professionals describing how they use mathematics in their work might be included. Parents are often eager to help their children learn when given the opportunity and guidance to do so. Include a simple game that could be played at home to reinforce children's learning. *Family Math* (Stenmark 1986) is an excellent source of such activities.

References

Supporting Documents

Children's Literature Bibliography

Adams, Barbara. *The Go-Around Dollar.* New York: Four Winds Press, 1992.

Adler, David. *3D, 2D, 1D.* New York: Crowell, 1975.

Aker, Suzanne. *What Comes in Two's, Three's & Four's?* New York: Simon & Schuster, 1990.

Aliki. *My Feet.* New York: HarperCollins, 1990.

Aliki. *My Hands,* New York: HarperCollins, 1990.

Allen, Pamela. *Who Sank the Boat?* New York: Putnam, 1985.

Birch, David. *The King's Chessboard.* New York: Dial Books for Young Readers, 1988.

Burns, Marilyn. *The One Dollar Word Riddle Book.* New Rochelle, NY: Cuisenaire, 1990.

Cribb, Joe. *Money.* New York: Knopf, 1990.

Crismann. *Hot Off the Press.* Minneapolis: Lerner, 1991.

Hoban, Tana. *26 Letters and 99 Cents.* New York: Greenwillow, 1987.

Maestro, Betsy and Giulio. *Dollars & Cents for Harriet.* New York: Crown, 1988.

Manes. *Make 4 Million Dollars by Next Thursday.* New York: Bantam, 1991.

Mathis, Sharon B. *The Hundred-Penny Box.* New York: Viking, 1975.

McKissack, Patricia. *A Million Fish . . . More or Less.* New York: Knopf, 1992.

Morrison and Eames. *Powers of Ten.* New York: Scientific American Library, 1983.

Myller, Rolf. *How Big Is a Foot?* New York: Macmillan, 1990.

Pittman, Helena C. *A Grain of Rice.* New York: Hastings House, 1986.

Rice, Eve. *Peter's Pockets.* New York: Greenwillow Books, 1989.

Russo, Marisabina. *The Line up Book.* New York: Greenwillow, 1986.

Schwartz, David M. *How Much Is a Million?* New York: Scholastic, 1987.

Schwartz, David M. *If You Made a Million.* New York: Lothrop, Lee & Shepard, 1989.

Viorst, Judith. *Alexander, Who Used to Be Rich Last Sunday.* New York: Macmillan, 1989.

Walters. *How Newspapers Are Made.* New York: Facts on File, 1989.

References

Associated Press. "Year Off to Bloody Start with $31.5 Billion Deficit." *Rocky Mountain News.* November 24, 1990, p.66.

Buxton, Laurie. *Mathematics for Everyone.* New York: Schocken Books, 1984.

Barratta-Lorton, Mary. *Mathematics Their Way.* Menlo Park, Calif.: Addison-Wesley Publishing Co., 1976, p. 66.

California Department of Education. *Mathematics Framework for California Public Schools.* Sacramento: California Department of Education, 1985.

California Department of Education. *Mathematics Model Curriculum Guide, K–8.* Sacramento: California Department of Education, 1987.

Cole, Robert. "A Wish for My Child." *Phi Delta Kappan.* November 1987, p. 178.

Conference Board of the Mathematical Sciences. *"The Mathematical Sciences Curriculum K–12: What Is Still Fundamental and What Is Not?"* Report to National Science Commission on Precollege Education in Mathematics, Science and Technology. Washington, D.C.: Conference Board of the Mathematical Sciences, 1982.

Crimmins, James A. *The Challenge of the Unknown.* New York: W.W. Norton & Co., 1986, pp. 214–217.

Dossey, John A., et al. *The Mathematics Report Card: Are We Measuring Up? Trends and Achievements Based on the 1986 National Assessment.* Princeton, NJ: Educational Testing Service, 1988.

Kamii, Constance. *Young Children Continue to Reinvent Arithmetic.* New York: Teachers College Press, 1989.

Kamii, Constance, and Barbara Ann Lewis. *"Achievement Tests in Primary Mathematics: Perpetuating Lower-Order Thinking."* Arithmetic Teacher. Reston, Va: National Council of Teachers of Mathematics, 1990, pp. 4–9.

Leutzinger, Larry P., and Myrna Bertheau. *"Making Sense of Numbers."* in New Directions for Elementary School Mathematics, ed. P. R. Trafton and A.P. Shulte. Reston, Va.: National Council of Teachers of Mathematics, 1989, pp. 111–122.

Moses, Barbara, Elizabeth Bjork and E. Paul Goldenberg. "Beyond Problem Solving: Problem Posing." in *Teaching and Learning Mathematics in the 1990s: 1990 Yearbook,* ed. T. J. Cooney and C.R. Hirsh. Reston, Va.: National Council of Teachers of Mathematics, 1990, pp. 82–91.

National Council of Teachers of Mathematics. *Curriculum and Evaluation Standards for School Mathematics.* Reston, Va.: National Council of Teachers of Mathematics, 1989.

National Council of Teachers of Mathematics. *Professional Standards for Teaching Mathematics.* Reston, Va.: National Council of Teachers of Mathematics, 1991.

National Research Council. *Everybody Counts.* Washington, D.C.: National Academy Press, 1989.

"It's Raining Pennies—But not from Heaven."*Newsweek,* January 7, 1991, p. 31.

Paulos, John Allen. *Innumeracy.* New York: Hill and Wang, 1988.

Richardson, Kathy. *A Look at Children's Thinking.* Norman, Okla.: Educational Enrichment Inc., 1990.

Stenmark, Jean Kerr, Virginia Thompson, and Ruth Cossey. *Family Math.* Berkeley: University of California, 1986.

Strands and Grade-Level Chart

Lessons:

Lessons	Numeration	Estimation	Number Operations	Measurement	Graphing/Statistics	Logic	Algebra	Patterns	Grade Level
Handfuls		■		■					1–3
Paces	■			■					1–3
The King's Foot	■	▢		■					1–3
Body Perimeters	■			■					K–3
Average Height	▢		▢	■					3–6
Tiles in Our Shoes	■	▢							1–3
Cover-Ups	■	■							1–3
Peter's Pockets	■		■						K–3
Weighing Pennies	▢			■					K–2
Pennies on Paper	■	▢							1–3
100 Links	▢			■					K–2
Make a Dollar	▢			■	▢				1–3
Things That Come In...	▢							▢	2–4
Build a Number	■								2–4
Measuring with Pennies	■		▢	■			▢		2–6
Dimes and Pennies	▢					■			1–6
Coin Combos	▢							▢	2–4
Grains of Rice	■	■	▢						3–8
The Richter Scale	■		▢	▢					3–8
A Million Blades of Grass	▢	■							4–8
A Dollar's Worth	▢		■				■	■	3–6
Newspaper Numbers	■								2–8
Daily Numbers	■	▢							1–8
Place-Value Graphing	■				■				3–8
Guess My Number	■					■			3–6
Number Search	■		▢			■			2–8
Place-Value Hockey	■								4–6
The Rounding Game	■	■							4–6
Make a Million	■	▢	■						4–8
How Many Seconds . . .	■	■	■					▢	4–8
Where Are the Big Numbers?	■	■	▢						4–8
You've Got the Answer	▢	■	■			▢			1–8
A Paper Million	■	■	■						5–8
Who's Greatest?	■		▢			▢	▢		3–6
Making Allowances	▢		■				▢	▢	3–8

■ Major Emphasis:

▢ Secondary Emphasis: